W9-BFI-522

Be Blessed!

E. S. Mohanj

Commendations for *Blessed by the Blood*

"This book serves as an effective tool for its readers. To discover the various blessings that one can receive through the blood of Jesus. Samuel clearly teaches the indispensable need of the blood of Jesus Christ in bringing blessing to any human."

— REV. DAVID MOHAN
New Life Assembly of God, India

"Dr. Samuel M. Ebenezer has masterfully written a refreshing book in which every page offers practical gems gleaned from his personal meditation encounters with God. These indispensable, foundational, timeless truths anchor every saint to stand firmly upon the impregnable, unassailable, and invincible foundation of Calvary!"

— DR. JEDIDIAH THAM
Living Lilies, Singapore

"In his newest book, *Blessed by the Blood*, Samuel M. Ebenezer has succinctly and cogently crafted a powerfully insightful and practical treatise on a truth foundational and fundamental to the Christian faith. His handling of this subject reveals the all-encompassing power contained in the blood of Jesus and its application to our everyday lives. Samuel Ebenezer pulls back the curtain, as it were, on what has remained for many believers a shrouded mystery. This is a must read for every disciple of Christ who desires an overcoming and victorious life!"

– REV. STEVE SCHUESSLER
Lighthouse Christian Fellowship, NJ

"Samuel M. Ebenezer has done a masterful job unpacking what the Bible has to say regarding the all-sufficient gift of our perfect and complete restoration and redemption made available to you through the blood of Christ. I'm sure you'll be blessed, encouraged, and forever grateful to God as you read and discover the remarkable provision found in what Christ has done for you on the cross of Calvary."

– PASTOR KENT HUMMEL
Good Shepherd Church, CO

"It is an honor to be able to call brother Samuel a great man of God, a wonderful evangelist, and a dear friend. *Blessed by the Blood* gives divine insight into God's Word. Brother Samuel's method of preaching and writing give deep revelation of God's Kingdom."

– PASTOR JEFF GANDY
Blondy Church of God, TN

"Blessed by the Blood has been presented in the most interesting and insightful manner. The blessings that we have received through Jesus offering His blood are clearly and carefully outlined in this book and I have found this book to be a positive message on Christ's atoning sacrifice. Christians and non-Christians with the aid of the Holy Spirit, should be able to easily comprehend the length, breadth, and the height of God's love written on the pages of this book. I believe everyone should gain a new appreciation for all that was involved in Jesus' suffering for our salvation."

– REV. JOHN D. JOHNSON
Bay Shore Assembly of God, NY

"This latest book of Minister Samuel M. Ebenezer is a powerful reminder of the wonder working power of the blood of Jesus. All who fully open their hearts to these daily meditations will experience the Eternal Priest Himself applying that blood to us, so we may live in the full power and blessing of the blood of the Lamb."

– PASTOR BRIAN AMATO
RiverLife Church, NJ

"Dr. Samuel M. Ebenezer has captured the complete effectiveness of the blood of Jesus in this book. He offers an extensive study on the benefits and blessings all believers are entitled to through the blood of Jesus Christ. While we sometimes struggle with various things during our lifetime, remembering what Christ has paid for, and made available because of His suffering, gives all of us a victory to look back to, a victory to live daily in, and a victory to look forward to upon our arrival in heaven!"

– STEVEN B. SMITH
Global Messenger Service, MO

"I was blessed as I read this book. Although there are many books on the effectiveness and the power of the blood of Jesus Christ, I find this book brings a different approach which is simple, understandable, and interesting because of its storytelling style that can cause any believer to apply it to his or her life and know how much and how effective the blood of Jesus Christ is in one's daily life. I would highly recommend this book to any believer who wants to receive and remain in the blessings of the Lord."

– REV. ROY MUTTIAH
Cornerstone Glory Centre, West Malaysia

"Dr. Samuel M. Ebenezer has written a book on the blood of Jesus. This is an important subject that all believers should know and know thoroughly. From the day the blood of Jesus trickled down the cross in Calvary, it became a living torrent available to all. To the believer, the blood is their sufficiency for a lifetime walk with Jesus. All their needs are met in the blood of Jesus. In *Blessed by the Blood*, Samuel has adequately and clearly expounded upon this through scholarship and a lifetime of experience guided and inspired by the Holy Spirit. I have no doubt that all who read this book will be richly blessed and reminded of their rich heritage in the blood so lovingly shed for us on the cross of Calvary."

– THIO GIM HOCK
City Missions Church, Singapore

Blessed by the Blood

*30 Revelations on the
Power and Blessings
of Jesus' Blood*

Samuel M. Ebenezer

Fedd Books
P.O. Box 341973
Austin, TX 78734

www.thefeddagency.com

Published in association with The Fedd Agency, Inc., a literary agency.

Unless otherwise indicated, all Scripture quotations are taken from the New King James Version®. Copyright © 1982 by Thomas Nelson. Used by permission. All rights reserved.

Scripture quotations marked (KJV) are taken from the King James Version of the Bible.

Scripture quotations marked (MSG) are taken from THE MESSAGE, copyright © 1993, 1994, 1995, 1996, 2000, 2001, 2002 by Eugene H. Peterson. Used by permission of NavPress. All rights reserved. Represented by Tyndale House Publishers, Inc.

Scripture quotations marked (NIV) are taken from the Holy Bible, New International Version®, NIV®. Copyright © 1973, 1978, 1984, 2011 by Biblica, Inc.™ Used by permission of Zondervan. All rights reserved worldwide. www.zondervan.com The "NIV" and "New International Version" are trademarks registered in the United States Patent and Trademark Office by Biblica, Inc.™

Scripture quotations marked (NLT) are taken from the Holy Bible, New Living Translation, copyright ©1996, 2004, 2015 by Tyndale House Foundation. Used by permission of Tyndale House Publishers, Inc., Carol Stream, Illinois 60188. All rights reserved.

Scripture quotations marked (AMP) are taken from the Amplified Bible Copyright © 1954, 1958, 1962, 1964, 1965, 1987 by The Lockman Foundation, La Habra, CA. All rights reserved. Used by Permission. www.lockman.org.

Scripture quotations marked (AMPC) are taken from the Amplified Bible, Classic Edition Copyright © 1954, 1958, 1962, 1964, 1965, 1987 by The Lockman Foundation, La Habra, CA. All rights reserved. Used by Permission. www.lockman.org.

Scripture quotations marked (ASV) are taken from the American Standard Version of the Bible.

Scripture quotations marked (CEV) are taken from the Contemporary English Version® Copyright © 1995 American Bible Society. All rights reserved.

Scripture quotations marked (GW) are taken from GOD'S WORD, a copyrighted work of God's Word to the Nations. Quotations are used by permission. Copyright 1995 by God's Word to the Nations. All rights reserved.

Scripture quotations marked (TLB) are taken from The Living Bible copyright © 1971 by Tyndale House Foundation. Used by permission of Tyndale House Publishers Inc., Carol Stream, Illinois 60188. All rights reserved. The Living Bible, TLB, and the The Living Bible logo are registered trademarks of Tyndale House Publishers.

ISBN: 978-1-949784-35-0
eISBN: 978-1-949784-36-7

Printed in the United States of America

First Edition 15 14 13 12 11 / 10 9 8 7 6 5 4 3 2

For the glory of God, I dedicate this book to my uncle, the late Mr. James Samuel, who led me to salvation.

Contents

foreword

This book lays an incredible foundation on the importance of the blood of Jesus and is written unlike any other by explaining the deep things of the Word. Samuel depicts well the necessity and power of why we need the blood; it is the "heart of the Gospel." He defends its legal right of holiness and explains why it was the final atonement. Samuel argues that "Until we, as sinners, have the experience of being saved by grace, we cannot truly fathom how precious the blood of Christ is." He even goes further in explaining how precious we are to God, "Each one of us is precious in His sight—irrespective of our status, color, race, religion or qualification." The precious blood of Christ, and the promises and favor that come with it, are available to each one of us to this day.

I particularly enjoyed the chapter on the blood of Jesus having a voice. Samuel paints a beautiful picture of the blood of Jesus, crying out for you! *Blessed by the Blood* will change the way a believer sees the blood and its power. It will give you a deeper appreciation for Christ and His sacrifice. Samuel exposes impactful truths that are always happening in our favor that most believers can't see. *Blessed by the Blood* reveals the forgiveness, victory, mercy, and peace that are always available. Samuel said it well when he said, "no matter why the curse has come upon us, our good Lord has made a way out of it." Every believer should read this book, if for nothing else than to fall in love again with the One who gave the greatest sacrifice known to the universe.

-Dr. Perry Stone

Founder of Perry Stone Ministries, VOE, OCI, ISOW

Introduction

In Exodus, we read that the Lord sent ten plagues to show His power and might to the Egyptians in order to make them set the Israelites free. Let's focus on the first plague and the last plague among the ten. We see in the first plague that God turned the waters of the Nile into blood so that it flowed over all of Egypt (Exodus 7:20-21). In the final plague, the Israelites were instructed to sacrifice an unblemished lamb and apply its blood on the doorposts. That night, they observed the very first Passover. When the Angel of death saw the blood, he passed over the Israelite homes; but the firstborn of every Egyptian was struck down. It is indeed interesting to note that the Israelites' battle for freedom started with blood, and it ended with blood.

However, in the first plague, while the Israelites merely saw the blood in the Nile, in the last plague, they had to apply the blood to be delivered. Similarly, the truth demonstrated here is that it is not enough just to see or know about the blood of Christ. We must apply it to our lives.

This blood brings us absolute liberty in every area of our lives.

The work of the blood of Jesus is not finished on the cross. It is working and continues to work. Satan and the powers of darkness tremble at the very mention of the words *"the blood of Jesus."* They know that this is the most powerful weapon working against them. Hence, it is important for us to know the different perspectives of Jesus' blood. The Bible offers a tremendous amount of insight on this subject.

> *When you start applying the blood of Jesus to situations, persons, and other obstacles, the blood will unlock all required blessings in your life.*

In the book of Hebrews, the blood of Jesus is also referred to as *"the blood of sprinkling"* (Hebrew 12:24). It is not in the past or present tense, rather it is in the continuous tense. That means that we can keep on applying His blood. When you say, "I sprinkle the blood of Jesus" or when you sprinkle water or oil claiming the blood of Jesus, it causes a change in the spiritual realm. This is not just a physical act, but rather a scriptural action that has spiritual significance. *When you start applying the blood of Jesus to situations, persons, and other obstacles, the blood will unlock all required blessings in your life.* This spiritual transformation will ultimately bring about a radical change in the physical realm.

Several years ago, I purchased an apartment after much deliberation. After I had paid an advance on the property, a colleague of mine pointed out that the number on the door of the apartment was 13/8. It is no secret that many people consider thirteen an unlucky number. It should be noted that many Indians consider eight as an unlucky number as well! My well-meaning colleague advised me to reconsider my decision.

Though I was briefly troubled, the Lord assured me through His word in Ephesians 1:20-22, that every demonic activity is subject to the power of Christ, and He has placed all of this under His feet.

I knew that the apartment's previous owners had performed many magic spells and incantations in this very place and that they were deep in debt. After I bought the apartment, I started to face financial difficulties of my own. My heart grew troubled again, and I began to ponder over the bold decision I had made. It was then that the Lord spoke to me from Leviticus 14:51-53, which records rituals from the Old Testament for atoning a house. The rituals included the application of the blood with hyssop, among other things. I decided to put this teaching into practical use.

Every day, I would walk around my new house speaking aloud and saying, "*Lord I sprinkle the precious blood You shed for us on every window, door post, and wall.*" I repeated this prayer every day—seven times a day. Apart from this, I also sprinkled water that was blessed as His precious blood all over the apartment—in faith! A few months later, a pastor visited our apartment. As he prayed, he exclaimed, "Brother Samuel, I see the blood of Jesus all over the place!"

Since then, I have been faithful in applying the blood of Jesus, using the declaration of my mouth, over my family, finances, health and property! Today, I can tell you that the same apartment has been a great blessing to me and to my family.

This book is the fruit of many years of study, research, and preaching of the Word. I have included many deep revelations as revealed to me by our wonderful Lord God. There are many real-life stories of how the blood of Jesus has changed lives and ministered to people.

In each chapter, there are five sections: key point, message, application, prayer, and reflection. This book is designed to help you understand the significance of the blood and apply it to your life. I offer this book so that you may easily and purposefully gain knowledge about the purpose and power in the blood of Jesus, and enjoy all the glorious blessings that come with it. You can apply the blood of Jesus in your life and receive the purchases it has made by faith.

I would strongly recommend that you make this a month-long challenge—to read and apply the teachings in this book at the pace of a chapter a day. This will help you meditate on the deeper aspects of this book and walk by them.

Let me now emphasize that the blood of Jesus does not work independently, but is knit together with the Word of God and the Person of the Holy Spirit. May the Spirit of the Lord reveal the depth of His blessings through the blood of Jesus and bless you abundantly as you read this book.

– Samuel M. Ebenezer

Part One

The Foundation of the Blood

Why Jesus' Blood?

"For God so loved the world that He gave His only begotten Son, that whoever believes in Him should not perish but have everlasting life. For God did not send His Son into the world to condemn the world, but that the world through Him might be saved."

— John 3:16-17

Key Point:

God our Creator, who is the very source of our life and blood, chose to shed His blood and be our final sacrificial lamb, as atonement for all our sins, for all eternity!

Message:

The blood of Jesus is the heart of the gospel. Before we expound the various blessings found in the blood of Jesus, let us understand the uniqueness of Jesus' blood. This will give us the much-needed, clear foundation upon which we can build our precepts.

So, what was the need for Jesus to come down to earth

and live as a man for thirty-three years? Why did He need to go through the very intense and most horrific experience of the cross? Why would Jesus, the very Son of God, have to shed His blood? The answer is plain. It was because of God's great, deep love for us. But the question remains: Why do we need the sacrifice of the blood of Jesus? What is the importance or significance of blood?

First, it is most essential that we understand blood. The most consistent and clearly prominent theme through the Bible, right from Genesis to Revelation, is blood. Leviticus 17:11 says, *"the very life of a man is in his blood."* The very basis of our salvation is in the blood of the author of our lives, Jesus Christ, the Son of God. *The born-again life of the believer is built on the foundation of Jesus' blood.*

In Genesis, our fore-parents, Adam and Eve, listened to the words of Satan, who was disguised as a snake, and disobeyed God's command. They ended up eating the forbidden fruit of the tree of the knowledge of good and evil; thus they—and all mankind—fell into sin. When a snake bites a person, the blood of the person is poisoned due to the snake's venom. Similarly, in the Garden of Eden, the sting of sin spiritually poisoned the blood of Adam and Eve. Being their descendants, our blood, too, has become spiritually stained and infected. This is further confirmed when David says in Psalm 51:5, *"Behold, I was brought forth in iniquity, and in sin my mother conceived me."*

> *The born-again life of the believer is built on the foundation of Jesus' blood.*

In the Old Testament times, there were two methods of atonement for sin. In the first category, the blood of animals (bulls, rams, goats, turtledoves, or young pigeons) was shed and offered as atonement for the sins of men (Leviticus 4:3-8, 5:6-10, 17-19, 19:21). When a person committed a sin, he had to choose a permitted animal or bird and bring it to the priest. The priest would then place his hands on the sacrifice and allow the sin of the person who brought the sacrifice to transfer into the animal. This animal was later slaughtered at the altar as atonement for that person's sin. The blood, thus shed, is the atonement for the sin committed by that person.

In the second category, if a person committed a very grave offense, such as murder, the blood of the very person who committed the sin had to be shed as atonement. Numbers 35:33 highlights this: *"for blood defiles the land, and no atonement can be made for the land, for the blood that is shed on it, except by the blood of him who shed it."*

In Luke 3:23-36, we see the genealogy of Jesus Christ. It was traced back not only to Adam but also to God Himself. *"Now Jesus Himself began His ministry at about thirty years of age, being (as was supposed) the son of Joseph, the son of Heli . . . the son of Enosh, the son of Seth, the son of Adam, the son of God."* From this genealogy, we get one clear fact: *God is the source of human blood.*

Back in Genesis, we see that God created Adam and Eve in His own image and likeness. God gave their blood to them, and He Himself was the blood's source. Acts 17:26 says, *"And He made from one [common origin, one source, one blood] all nations of men to settle on the face of the earth . . ."* (AMPC). The same God, who originally gave life to man when He created Adam also sent His only begotten Son as a Lamb, without spot or blemish, to redeem mankind with His precious blood (1 Peter 1:19).

In other words, instead of us, the offenders, having to shed our blood as atonement for our offenses and sins, our God—the Creator of our life, the very source of our life-blood—shed His blood to atone for our sins. His sacrifice does not only atone for the sins of a particular category; His blood atones for all the sins of all mankind.

In medicine, when a man's blood becomes totally impure and poisoned, one of the main courses of treatment is a blood transfusion. Being born as sinners, with blood that has been tainted by sin, we too need pure, sinless blood to be transfused into us. Christ's sinless blood removes the stain of sin in us and gives us a new lease on life. The Bible says that *"without the shedding of blood there is neither release from sin* and *its guilt* nor *the remission of the due* and *merited punishment for sins"* (Hebrews 9:22, AMPC).

Application:

Now because of God's great sacrifice of blood, there is no more need for the sacrifice of animals or birds as originally decreed by God. Jesus' sacrifice nullified the need for the shedding of blood, either of an animal or a human, by any sinner. 1 John 2:2 reminds us of this truth: *"And He [that same Jesus] is the propitiation for our sins [the atoning sacrifice that holds back the wrath of God that would otherwise be directed at us because of our sinful nature—our worldliness, our lifestyle]; and not for ours alone, but also for [the sins of all believers throughout] the whole world"* (AMP).

God, who created us, has provided eternal redemption through His own blood. We need no other sacrifice to atone for our sins because Christ has paid the price for us. Acts 20:28 says, *"the church of God which He purchased with His own blood."*

What a great gift He has given us through His blood!

Prayer:

Dear Lord, how deep is Your love for me that You CHOSE to shed Your lifeblood for me! Thank You for taking my place and for dying to atone for my sins. I accept this great gift, and I thank You for being my Savior. In the One and Only name of my Lord Jesus, I pray. Amen!

Reflection:

Write in your words the reason why God chose His son, Jesus, as the atoning sacrifice for the whole world.

Is there any other way God could have worked to save mankind?

The Holy Blood

*"But with the precious **blood of Christ**, a lamb*
__without blemish or defect__."

— 1 Peter 1:19 (NIV, emphasis added)

Key Point:

Our salvation was purchased with the most holy, flawless blood of Jesus Christ, our sacrificial lamb without blemish, who lived His life as a blameless man, and willingly gave up His life for us at the time appointed by God the Father.

Message:

When we read the Word of God, we see in any ceremonial sacrifices that the blood had to come from an animal without any blemish. This was required by the Holy God, who is perfect in all His ways (Exodus 12:5; Leviticus 1:10, 22:20). The blood had to be flawless to be able to serve as atonement for the sins of a man. The priest had to examine the sacrifice meticulously before it was offered, making sure that the animal was indeed without flaw or blemish. Similarly, the blood that was required to atone the sins of mankind, had to be flawless, sinless, pure blood. *Our God whom we worship is a Holy God, and He requires holiness.*

Jesus Christ, the Son of God, came into this world to live the life of a man. When Jesus came to John the Baptist, John said of Him, *"Behold! The Lamb of God who takes away the sin of the world"* (John 1:29). Although Jesus took on the form of a mortal, He led a holy life without sin. He even challenged his enemies saying, *"Which of you convicts Me of sin?"* (John 8:46). Though they tried to find fault with Him, not one of His enemies could find any sin in Jesus' life.

When Jesus stood accused before the judgment seat of Pontius Pilate, Pilate's wife sent word to him. She conveyed to him, *"Have nothing to do with that just Man, for I have suffered many things today in a dream because of Him"* (Matthew 27:19). God revealed to Pilate's wife through a dream that Jesus was righteous in the sight of God.

After this, Pontius Pilate further examined Jesus, but he could find no fault in Him (Luke 23:14; John 19:6). Pilate openly declared this truth to the crowds that were gathered there. However, when the chief priests, elders, and the people shouted out for Jesus' blood, demanding that He should be crucified, Pilate yielded to them. He then symbolically

> *Our God whom we worship is a Holy God, and He requires holiness.*

washed his hands before the multitude saying, *"I am inno-cent of the blood of this just Person"* (Matthew 27:24). Pontius Pilate, who examined Jesus, could find no sin in Him and proclaimed that Jesus was a righteous person.

The disciples, who walked and lived with Jesus over a period of three years, also testified to the sinless life of Jesus. Peter says, *"He committed no sin, and no deceit was found in His mouth"* (1 Peter 2:22, NIV). John says of Jesus, *"In Him is no sin"* (1 John 3:5). Even Judas Iscariot, who betrayed Jesus for thirty silver coins said, *"I have sinned by betraying innocent blood"* (Matthew 27:4).

One of the two thieves who were crucified along with Jesus declared, *"This man has done nothing wrong"* (Luke 23:41). The centurion who crucified Jesus proclaimed Jesus' innocence after Jesus breathed His last, saying, *"Truly this was the Son of God!"* (Matthew 27:54).

Above all, God Himself bore witness to Jesus' in-nocence. In the book of Isaiah, we read prophesies that spoke of Christ. Isaiah 53:9 says, *"He had done no violence, nor was any deceit in His mouth."* God, in Isaiah 53:11, refers to Christ as *"My righteous servant."* Just take a moment to ponder the innocence of Jesus.

We have seen that our Lord Jesus Christ led a pure life while He was in the world. But during His time on earth, we know that the devil tried in many ways, and by many means, to kill Jesus. *Though Christ was beaten fiercely and every part of His body was tortured, He did not die right away, I believe, because Jesus had no sin in Him.*

The Scripture says, *"For the wages of sin is death"* (Romans 6:23). If a man does not commit sin, will he yet die? If our Lord had indeed led a sinful life like us, I believe He would have died when the Roman soldiers whipped Him so mercilessly.

He made this very clear in His own words. He said that no one could take His life. *"No one takes it from Me, but I lay it down of Myself. I have power to lay it down, and I have power to take it again. This command I have received from My Father"* (John 10:18).

He laid down His life on the cross to conquer the final enemy—death! We can see this in 1 Corinthians 15:25, 55-57: Christ has put his enemies under his feet and has freed us from the sting of death. In Luke 23:46 we read, *"Jesus called out with a loud voice, 'Father, into Your hands I commit my spirit.' When He had said this, He breathed His last."*

He gave up His life at the time appointed by God, so that God's plan for man's redemption could be carried out. Neither the devil nor man could scheme to take His life away from Him before that hour.

This proves that Jesus led a sin-free life, and so, His blood was unblemished and flawless. He was not subject to death like the sinful blood of a normal man would have been. After Jesus gave up His Spirit on the cross, the veil in the temple was torn from the top to bottom (Matthew 27:50-51). This significant incident also indicates that His blood, shed for us at the appointed hour, satisfied all the requirements of Almighty God for the purchase of our salvation.

The blood of Jesus was indeed holy.

Application:

Through Jesus' blood, we are made holy when we have faith in Him. Though we are not sinless or flawless, we are made holy through the covering of Jesus' blood. Our faith in his atoning sacrifice allows us the privilege to partake of His holiness in our lives. Thus, His holy blood enables us to be acceptable in the sight of our Holy God.

Prayer:

Dear Lord, thank You for your sacrifice on the cross. I know You lived a holy and blameless life, just so You could be a blemish-free sacrifice on the cross for ME! I am so grateful for Your grace that bestows Your holiness in my life. You did this for me at Calvary. I am Yours—purchased by Your blood. In the hallowed name of Jesus, I pray. Amen!

Reflection:

Is it possible for any human being to obtain the standard of holiness required by God?

How do you conclude that Jesus' blood is holy?

How can we live a holy life while still being imperfect people?

The Precious Blood

"Knowing that you were not redeemed with corruptible things . . .
*but with **the precious blood of Christ**,*
as of a lamb without blemish and without spot."

– 1 Peter 1:18-19 (emphasis added)

Key Point:

When we truly understand the great sacrifice of Christ for our salvation, we become aware of how precious His blood really is and how precious we are in the eyes of God.

Message:

What is considered the most valuable substance in this universe? According to the Bible, it is not silver, gold, platinum, or even diamonds, but the blood of Jesus Christ, the Son of the Living God. *Indeed, if things bought with corruptible articles such as silver and gold hold such great value, how much more valuable are we who are purchased by the invaluable blood of the Lamb on Calvary?*

In the Parables of the Hidden Treasure and the Pearl (Matthew 13:44-46), we read a story that Jesus used as an illustration to exhibit the great value of the Kingdom of God. Jesus speaks of a merchant who traded in pearls and other precious articles. When this merchant found a fine and precious pearl of great value, he sold everything he had in order to purchase this single pearl. In our lives, we can draw a parallel to this parable. When we

> *Indeed, if things bought with corruptible articles such as silver and gold hold such great value, how much more valuable are we who are purchased by the invaluable blood of the Lamb on Calvary?*

hold something very dear to us, or when we place a lot of value on something, we are inclined to give up everything we can in order to gain it, for it becomes irreplaceable to us. We must learn this great truth: Jesus is this pearl of great value. He is precious and worth everything we have to offer him.

Peter is, arguably, one of the most famous of the twelve disciples. He was an ordinary fisherman when Jesus entered into His life. After spending several years with Jesus, Peter was changed into a fisher of men. When Peter recognized Jesus' great power and worth, He dropped everything—left everything behind—and followed Jesus. He witnessed many miracles first-hand. He saw healing every day, and he walked and lived with Jesus Christ. Witnessing Jesus' life and behavior and the supernatural power He demonstrated, had Peter convinced in his spirit so much that he said, *"You are the Christ, Son of the living God"* (Matthew 16:16).

However, on the road to Calvary, when Jesus was arrested and taken to the house of the High Priest, Peter was the one who denied Him thrice before hastily leaving the courtyard. It is my belief that Peter did not witness the brutal flogging and unjust trial of Jesus, as he was no longer on the scene after his betrayal. When Jesus appeared to Peter after His resurrection, Jesus extended grace to Peter, forgiving him for his betrayal and giving him a critical purpose in furthering the kingdom of God (John 21). Later in his life, Peter speaks of the "precious" blood of Jesus with great fondness, and I think this is because he has experienced the grace of God extended to him only through the blood of Christ.

Most often, it is during adverse situations that we realize what or who holds the highest value to us. We do not see how precious health is until we get sick, or realize how important food is until we suffer the pangs of hunger. And we do not realize the value of family, or that of friends, until we have lost someone we love. Our times of poverty or lack teach us the value of prosperity; a situation of unemployment may teach us the preciousness of work. And it holds true that we do not realize how precious our freedom is, until we experience the cruelty of slavery. *Until we, as sin-*

> *Until we, as sinners, have the experience of being saved by grace, we cannot truly fathom how precious the blood of Christ is.*

ners, have the experience of being saved by grace, we cannot truly fathom how precious the blood of Christ is.

The Bible says in 1 Corinthians 6:20 *"You were bought at a price . . ."* This price was the matchless, precious blood of Jesus. Furthermore, Romans 3:23-24 says, *"For all have sinned and fall short of the glory of God, and all are justified freely by his grace through the redemption that came by Christ Jesus"* (NIV). The cost of our redemption and our salvation from sin was the precious blood of Jesus.

If the Creator who made you, me, and the whole universe shed His precious blood for us, how precious we are to Him!

Application:

Each one of us is precious in His sight—irrespective of our status, color, race, religion or qualification. We are SO precious to God! We are not only precious in His sight, but He has also bestowed us with honor (Isaiah 43:4). This thought really lifted my spirit. I hope it does the same for you.

The Almighty God, Creator of the entire universe, has placed such great value on us! He has chosen to purchase us through the precious blood of His own, beloved Son. Therefore, let us be grateful and faithful for the precious life that our Lord has given, and let the name of the Lord be glorified in this world through our lives.

Prayer:

Dear Lord, Your blood is so precious. It is indeed a privilege to know and understand the value of Your blood. Thank You that You deemed me worthy of this precious, priceless blood. I pray that Your blood would work in me and through me so that I may be a channel of this gift of love, grace, and mercy to all mankind! In the precious name of Jesus I pray, Amen!

Reflection:

Do you consider the blood of Jesus of great value in your life? If so, how do you preserve this?

In what areas of your life do you feel unworthy or worthless? Pray the precious blood of Christ over those things and be reminded of your worth in Him.

The Everlasting Power In Jesus' Blood

*"Now may the God of peace, **who through the blood of the eternal covenant brought back from the dead our Lord Jesus**, that great Shepherd of the sheep. . ."*

– Hebrews 13:20 (NIV, emphasis added)

Key Point:

When we exercise faith in the finished work of Jesus and apply His blood over our challenges, the blood of Jesus, which is everlasting, can redeem us—not just our souls that were dead in sin. The blood can even deliver us from adverse situations during our earthly life. The blood will never lose its power!

Message:

The blood of Jesus was shed on Calvary many, many years

ago, but it never loses its power. The blood of Jesus gives strength to the weary. It reaches to the highest mountain and touches down to the deepest valley. It soothes all doubts and calms all fears.

Human blood and animal blood are constantly changing, and after its lifespan, the blood has no value. However, the blood of Jesus has more to offer than meets the microscope! This is why we read in Hebrews 9:12: "*He did not enter by means of the blood of goats and calves; but he entered the Most Holy Place once for all by His own blood, thus obtaining eternal redemption*" (NIV). Jesus, the eternal High Priest, brought us redemption though His own blood that He shed. He created a way for us to reach Heaven. His death did not cause His blood to lose its power. Instead, it gained power and became a powerful weapon by which man can be liberated from the power of death!

> *His everlasting life, which is in His blood, never loses its power.*

His blood is unique and not mere human blood. His blood will never lose its power.

When Jesus came down to earth, the Bible says that He was God Himself, manifested in the flesh (1 Timothy 3:16; Romans 9:5). The source of Jesus' blood is God Himself. Acts 20:28 clearly states that God purchased the church of God with His own blood. The Alpha and the Omega, the first and the last, became human in the form of Jesus and so *His everlasting life, which is in His blood, never loses its power.* It has an everlasting vigor that is enough for the past, the present, and the future.

In the book of Revelation, John sees a vision of the slain Lamb of God, and exclaims that the victory was won by the blood of the Lamb (Revelation 12:11). This victory is ongoing; even after the death of the Lamb, who was Jesus the Christ, the blood still accomplishes victory!

The blood of Christ works on our very conscience—deep within—and purifies it. How much more power and life does the blood of Christ hold! Even two thousand years after His death and resurrection, His blood continues to work to purify and sanctify us.

It was the blood of Jesus that raised Him from the dead. How remarkable that the blood of the very person who died had the power within it to raise Him from the dead! *Every drop of blood shed by Christ on the cross has the power to raise people from the dead—spiritually and even physically—even today! This life-restoring power of Christ's blood will never change!*

Some years ago, my dad and mom went to a lady's home to pray. When they reached her home, the lady told them that her son had picked up a big knife and wanted to kill his sisters. Seeing this, the lady quickly locked her daughters in a room. The son was furious with her. In addition to this, the lady told my parents that she and her

> *Every drop of blood shed by Christ on the cross has the power to raise people from the dead—spiritually and even physically—even today! This life-restoring power of Christ's blood will never change!*

husband quarreled constantly, and there was no peace in their home.

My mother remembered reading in one of my books about how the blood of Jesus can cleanse a house from demonic powers. She told the lady to apply the blood of Jesus in her house.

The next time they visited, my parents saw the words, "*Victory in the blood of Jesus*" written on every doorpost in the lady's home. She believed with all her heart that she would have deliverance through the blood of Jesus. As it turned out, our Lord truly brought victory to that family. The children are now highly educated and doing well in life. She and her husband are still together and remain strong in Christ. I believe that the power in the blood of Jesus transformed their adverse situation and restored all their broken relationships in that family.

Application:

Remember, it is His blood and His Spirit which raised Jesus from the grave on the third day (Hebrews 13:20; Romans 8:11). If the blood of Jesus could raise the mutilated, marred and disfigured dead body of Jesus from the tomb, the same blood can raise you up and out of any situation that is bringing you down.

The blood of Jesus has the power to restore any situation in your life. And we never have to fear that the effects and power of Jesus' blood will wear off because His blood is eternally powerful. We are made strong through the everlasting blood of Christ.

Prayer:

Dear Lord, how amazing You are! How marvelous is Your blood that it can deliver me not just from eternal death, but also rescue me from my problems while I am on earth. I know that time and space don't change the power of the blood! Let Your ever-exciting and ever-living blood flow into me. And by its everlasting power, raise me up from all my adverse situations. In the everlasting name of Jesus, I pray. Amen!

Reflection:

Why is Jesus' blood effective in our lives even today?

What can the blood of Jesus accomplish in your life today?

The Voice of Jesus' Blood

*"And to Jesus, the Mediator of a new covenant [uniting God and man], **and to the sprinkled blood, which speaks [of mercy]**, a better and nobler and more gracious message than the blood of Abel [which cried out for vengeance]."*

—Hebrews 12:24 (AMP, emphasis added)

Key Point:

The blood of Jesus, which purchased our salvation so long ago, "cries out" on our behalf even today—and brings to us forgiveness, victory, peace, grace, mercy, blessings and even more!

Message:

Cain and Abel, the brothers who were the world's first case of sibling rivalry, both brought the work of their hands before the Lord. Cain brought the produce of the land that he had cultivated, and Abel brought the first-born of his flock. But God, who sees the heart of all mankind, accepted the offering that Abel brought yet rejected

Cain's offering. Stirred up by anger and jealousy, Cain killed his brother, and then pretended as though nothing had happened.

Following this incident, God then said to Cain, *"Where is Abel your brother?"* to which Cain answered, *"I do not know. Am I my brother's keeper?"* When He heard Cain's cold, dismissive response, the Lord asked, *"What have you done? The voice of your brother's blood cries out to Me from the ground"* (Genesis 4:2-10). Blood has a voice that can cry out and make petition to God even after death, and this voice reaches the presence of God.

There is another incident in the Bible that speaks of the voice of blood. In 2 Samuel 21, we see that during the reign of King David, there was a severe famine in the land of Israel. The famine lasted all of three years. When King David enquired the reason from the Lord, He replied that it was because of the "bloodthirsty house of Saul." Saul had wronged the Gibeonites, and in return the Lord demanded that blood be repaid for blood.

The Gibeonites were a group of people descended from the Amorites. While the other inhabitants of Canaan rose up against Israel, the Gibeonites cunningly used a different strategy. They mounted their donkeys and made themselves look like worn-out travelers from afar. Their ruse worked, and the people of Israel struck a treaty to protect them without consulting with the Lord. When the deception of the Gibeonite delegation was found out, the Israelites of Joshua's generation knew that if they broke their oath to the Gibeonites, they would anger the Lord.

And so, they chose instead to subject the Gibeonites to a life of hard labor. They decided to let them live as slaves to the Israelites for generations to come.

During the time of King Saul's reign, due to the zeal for the children of Israel and Judah, the Gibeonites were put to death at the direction of the King (2 Samuel 21:2). This caused a curse to fall on Israel, which resulted in the famine. In short, the "blood of the slain Gibeonites" stood as a testament against the house of Israel and interfered with their well-being. To remedy this situation, and to put an end to the famine, seven sons of King Saul were put to death. We see this recorded in 2 Samuel 21:6. It was only after 'blood was repaid for blood,' that the land of Israel was healed.

Jesus also made this point very clear in Luke 11:50-51: *"That the blood of all the prophets which was shed from the foundation of the world may be required of this generation, from the blood of Abel to the blood of Zechariah who perished between the altar and the temple. Yes, I say to you, it shall be required of this generation."*

This illustrates very clearly that human blood, which is unlawfully shed, makes a cry for vengeance unto God. The blood of man has power as he is created in the very image of God. Even today, we see much blood that is spilled unlawfully. There are wars, family feuds, communal riots, and individual biases that cause bloodshed. This too reaches the throne of God. This is one of the reasons why there are generational curses; human blood that was unlawfully spent, even if it were decades ago, still cries out bitterly for it to be avenged.

If the blood of Abel and the blood of the Gibeonites, which were cases of human bloodshed, can make petition before God in this manner, how much more will the blood of Christ, the Lamb of God without blemish, cry out! *Jesus did not die on the cross so that He might bring condemnation on us. Instead, He died so that we may be liberated from the curses of sin and death.*

When we contrast the messages conveyed by the unjustly shed blood of Abel against the sacrificial blood of Christ, we see how, though they were both innocent whose blood was shed, what their blood speaks is so different!

- The blood of Abel cried out in condemnation, while the blood of Jesus speaks forgiveness.
- The blood of Abel cried out for justice and vengeance, but the blood of Jesus delivers a message of grace and mercy.
- The blood of Abel cried out in despair, but the blood of Jesus declares victory and peace.
- The blood of Abel was a voice of accusation, but the blood of Jesus is a voice of reconciliation.
- The blood of Abel cried out a curse, while the blood of Jesus speaks blessing.

King David had to take action to ensure that the blood of the Gibeonites was avenged. He brought justice to the Gibeonites for the injustice that was meted out to them years before. His bloodshed avenged the unjust bloodshed that Saul caused.

But the blood of Christ that was shed does not need to be avenged. Instead, it avenges us! It ensures our redemption. By His completed work on the cross, we have gained acceptance in the sight of God. Christ's

> *Jesus did not die on the cross so that He might bring condemnation on us. Instead, He died so that we may be liberated from the curses of sin and death.*

blood has provided for our salvation, it has delivered us from curse, and it has unlocked our blessings. And it is still calling out to all those who don't believe!

Indeed, the blood of Christ does not speak against us, but speaks for us so that we may receive God's abundant blessings upon our lives.

Application:

We are avenged through the blood of Christ. We no longer are slaves to sin and death, but we are liberated. Christ's blood speaks mercy and grace over every area of our lives. We don't have to fear condemnation, accusations, or curses; rather, we can rejoice in the blessing of salvation. Come to the blood that was shed on Calvary to unlock your blessings today!

Prayer:

Dear Lord, I am so grateful today that Your blood still cries out for sinners like me! Thank You that You are ever interceding for me. Let the voice of your blood unlock all the blessings in my life. I love You Lord, because You loved me first—so much that You stand in the gap even today. In the wonderful name of Jesus, I pray. Amen.

Reflection:

What would your blood speak if you died today?

What is the voice of Jesus' blood on your behalf?

Part Two

The Redemption

The Blood That fulfilled God's Law

"When God speaks of 'A new covenant'
He makes the first one obsolete. And whatever is
becoming obsolete (out of use, annulled) and growing
old is ready to disappear . . ."

– Hebrews 8:13 (AMP)

Key point:

Jesus Christ, our sacrificial Lamb, fulfilled all the laws of the old covenant through his sacrifice and bloodshed on the cross. We are saved by His grace through our faith and acceptance of this blood sacrifice.

Message:

The Old Testament prescribes a variety of rules and edicts, all of which had to be followed in order to meet the mandate prescribed by Almighty God. The New Testament, on the other hand, is simpler. *The New Testament's pivotal point is salvation.*

This salvation is through God's grace and through our faith in the death and resurrection of our Lord Jesus Christ. Often, there are healthy debates on whether the Old Testament, with its many laws, is still applicable to the

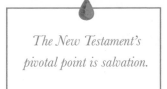

The New Testament's pivotal point is salvation.

New Testament Christian. Jesus answers this predicament with a simple statement found in Matthew 5:17: *"Do not think that I came to destroy the Law or the Prophets. I did not come to destroy but to fulfill."* Jesus was the only person capable of following and fulfilling all the laws of the Old Testament. Jesus lived a life that fulfilled all the requirements of the laws right from the beginning of his life on this earth. Luke 2:21 says that He was circumcised according to the law on the eighth day. Moreover, the Old Testament foreshadows the events fulfilled in and through the life of Christ in the New Testament. And so, the practices prescribed as part of the Mosaic Law, have a Messianic significance.

When God created man and other creatures on the earth, the "life blood" started to flow in them, bringing their forms to life. In the case of man, when the eternal breath of God that gave life was infused into him, man's heart started to beat for the first time, and blood started to course through his body.

At the fall of man, however, this blood was tainted by sin. Therefore, in order to cleanse it, a blood sacrifice was needed. The blood of sheep and cattle could never erase the sins of all mankind. As it is recorded in Hebrews 10:1, *"For the Law, having a shadow of the good things to come, and not the very image of the things, can never with these same sacrifices, which they offer continually year by year, make those who approach perfect."* This clearly shows us that the periodic sacrifices as prescribed by Moses were a mere foreshadow of the Lamb of God who would be slain for the sins of all human kind (Revelation 5:9).

When we read the scriptures detailing the Mosaic Law, we see that there are many offerings that are explained in detail. The offerings were made as atonement for sin and also as an act of worship unto God. The prescribed offerings were:

- **Burnt Offerings**: Select animals were offered as an expression of utter surrender to the Lord, and also as penance for unintentional sin (Leviticus 1; 6:8-13; 8:18-21; 16:24).
- **Grain Offerings**: The part of the harvest was offered as a token of thanksgiving to the Lord for His goodness (Leviticus 2; 6:14-23).
- **Peace Offering**: Certain animals were offered as an expression of worship, with a communal act of sharing. Vow offerings and free-will offerings were also made to the Lord (Leviticus 3; 7:11-34).
- **Sin Offering**: Bulls, goats, and lambs, as well as flour, were offered according to the social standing of the person seeking forgiveness for defilement or sin (Leviticus 4; 5:1-13; 6:24-30; 8:14-17; 16:3-22).

- **Trespass Offering**: A ram was offered for unintentional sins, and for overstepping the Lord's commands (Leviticus 5:14-19; 6:1-7; 7:1-6).

Apart from these, every day in the morning and evening, a lamb was offered as a sin offering unto the Lord. On the Sabbath and on festival days, additional animals were offered.

One significant festival day was The Day of Atonement, also referred to as Yom Kippur (Leviticus 16:20-22). On the Day of Atonement, which was observed once a year, two identical goats were chosen. Then, it was determined by the casting of lots, as to which one would be the "goat for the sacrifice" and which would be the "scapegoat." The goat that was chosen for the sacrifice was slain on the brazen altar as a blood sacrifice and as sin offering for the offenses of the entire congregation.

The scapegoat was then brought to the High Priest, who would then tie a scarlet thread made of wool across its horns before sending it away into the wilderness. Rabbinical traditions show that this signified that the scapegoat would carry evil far away from the Israelite camp. He would eventually return to the Devil from whom all evil originates. A piece of this scarlet thread was also nailed to the door of the temple. It was said that when the scapegoat died, the scarlet thread on the door of the temple would turn white. This indicated the forgiveness of their sins, and the dismissal of evil from their midst.[1] This may be the reason Isaiah the prophet says in Isaiah 1:18, *"Though your sins are like scarlet, they shall be as white as snow; though they are red like crimson, they shall be as wool."*

As we established earlier, the Old Testament foreshadows things that were later fulfilled in the New Testament—like the two identical goats, which were offered during Yom Kippur. An amazing parallel can be drawn in the atonement sacrifice of Jesus. Pilate asked the crowd whether they wanted to free Jesus or Barabbas. Barabbas, a convicted prisoner who was on trial at the same time as Jesus, was released at the time of Jesus' crucifixion. This is significant because Barabbas was the "son of the sinful father" while Jesus, was the Son of the Holy Father. Jesus, the lamb of God, was sacrificed like the sacrificial goat for the sins of the entire world in order to fulfill all God's law. Barabbas, on the other hand, walked free, but he was still laden with sin. He was the scapegoat. And so, here we can draw an unusual and interesting parallel. Barabbas, who was the "son of the sinful father" and Jesus, who was the Son of the Holy Father, each fulfilled his destiny. This is what is written in 2 Corinthians 5:21: *"For He made Him who knew no sin to be sin for us, that we might become the righteousness of God in Him."* Christ became sin for us. Barabbas, on the other hand, walked free, but he was still laden with sin. He was the scapegoat. As humans, we are no better than Barabbas, but we are not without hope.

Application:

In Colossians 2:14, we read, *"having canceled the charge of our legal indebtedness, which stood against us and condemned us; he has taken it away, nailing it to the cross"* (NIV). This means that sin no longer has any legal claim over our life. The blood of Christ that was shed on the cross has eradicated all punishment that was due to us for violating all God's law.

The great blood sacrifice of Christ shed for us on the cross has fulfilled all the Mosaic Law. We can live out of the freedom and grace that has come to us through Jesus' sacrifice. John 1:16-17 reveals this truth: *"And of His fullness we have all received, and grace for grace. For the law was given through Moses,* but *grace and truth came through Jesus Christ."*

Prayer:

Dear Lord, because of Your grace and sacrifice, I am saved! Thank You for eradicating all the legal indebtedness that was against me. It is Your blood that fulfilled all the laws on my behalf. I accept this great sacrifice of the Lamb of God, and declare that I am bought by Your blood and I am Yours! In the gracious name of our Savior, Lord Jesus Christ, I pray. Amen!

Reflection:

Will you be able to fulfill all the laws in the Old Testament? If not, what was the purpose of the laws?

What does the fact that Jesus fulfilled God's law mean for us?

The Blood of Jesus Redeems

*"Knowing that you were not **redeemed** with corruptible things, like silver or gold, from your aimless conduct received by tradition from your fathers, but **with the precious blood of Christ**, as of a lamb without blemish and without spot."*

– 1 Peter 1:18-19 (emphasis added)

Key Point:

The blood of Jesus has paid the *full* penalty for all our sins. No one can condemn us. We are completely redeemed. Satan no longer has any power over us, because we have been purchased AND redeemed by God!

Message:

Adam and Eve succumbed to the cunning of the devil and violated God's command by eating the forbidden fruit. They became slaves to the sin. Sin had dominion not only in their life, but also in their future generations. That is why we commit certain sins almost mechanically, however hard we may try to avoid them. The devil and sin overcome us and hold us under their control. Some of this may be beyond what we can fathom, but the truth is that until we are washed by the blood of Jesus, our life will be under the reign of the devil. *The personal experience of salvation is what breaks the hold that the devil has over us. Jesus has redeemed us from Satan's hold.*

Salvation means saving or redeeming, and in order to explain the power of redemption, I would like to narrate a story.

Let's say that a man accidentally leaves a very expensive watch on a table. His friend notices this and deliberates about whether to take it for himself or to return it. Satan utilizes this opportunity and encourages the friend to take the watch for himself. The man chides himself saying, "I cannot take this watch! God has created me in His likeness, and that means that I possess God's own attributes. Just like God, I cannot steal, kill, destroy and tell lies."

> *The personal experience of salvation is what breaks the hold that the devil has over us. Jesus has redeemed us from Satan's hold.*

Satan, on hearing these arguments, tempts the man further saying, "Since you feel guilty about this dishonest act, **let me lend you MY attributes** which include a disposition to steal, kill and destroy" (John 10:10b). Having borrowed these attributes of Satan, the man ventures to steal his friend's watch. However, in the due course of time, his own conscience gets the better of him. The Lord convicts him in a still, small voice and encourages Him to be truthful and not a liar like the devil, who is the father of all lies (John 8:44). He is soon pricked by guilt, and he decides to own up to his friend, and return the watch.

He goes to his friend's house and gives back the watch, and apologizes for his transgression. Though the watch, which belongs to his friend, can be returned, the attributes borrowed from Satan cannot be returned so easily. While the physical aspects of this transfer are easy to comprehend, ***the spiritual attributes now embedded within the blood of the person*** can never be fully understood. He could not return the attributes borrowed from Satan, as the Word says, *"the borrower is slave to the lender"* (Proverbs 22:7, NIV). Sin has corrupted the very character of man and made us less like God, and more like the fallen.

But God also made a way for this! The debt for this borrowed attribute of sin from Satan is canceled by the divine blood of the Lamb, who shed it willingly for us. We have already seen that the blood of Jesus has been shed for the atonement of all our sins. Jesus, the creator of the Universe, came and shed His blood, paid all our debts and set us free. The Word says in John 8:36, *"So if the Son sets you free, you will be free indeed." Jesus has paid all our debts in the Spiritual realm; the transaction is complete and we are free.*

When speaking about God's forgiveness, there are two words that are often used interchangeably. One is ***remission,*** and the other is ***redemption.*** However, these two words have different meanings. Remission means "paid the penalty" while redemption means "recovered." The following example will help you understand these concepts better:

When we go to a store, we buy an article by paying its price at the cash counter. After paying for it, we need to collect the article and take it with us. We claim ownership. If we forget to take possession of the article, then it remains at the store. Though you have paid for the item, since you have not actually taken it with you, it does not belong to you. It is not until you actually claim it that the article becomes yours. Similarly, when Jesus shed His blood on the cross, He not only paid the penalty on our behalf, but has also claimed and redeemed us from the clutches of Satan. Our salvation was purchased by the currency of His blood, and we were spiritually taken from Satan's control.

It says in 1 Peter 1:18-19 that we have been redeemed by the precious blood of Christ. Jesus declared just before

> *Jesus has paid all our debts in the Spiritual realm; the transaction is complete and we are free.*

He gave up His Spirit, "It is finished!" (John 19:30). The Greek word for this statement is "tetelestai." In accounting terms, it means "paid in full." The sinless blood of Christ has paid the *full* debt we owe for all our sins. Our redemption is not temporary, but eternal (Hebrews 9:12). Moreover, Acts 20:28 says that we have been purchased by His blood. This means the blood of Jesus is the heavenly currency that was paid by God in order to redeem us. We are completely free since Jesus has atoned for *all* our sins. Now we belong to our Lord Jesus (Isaiah 43:1). The new owner has redeemed us, and the old owner has no authority over us.

Romans 6:14 says, *"For sin shall not have dominion over you . . ."* Therefore, sin and its consequences can never overcome us. The blood of Jesus not only paid off all the penalties of our sin, but also redeemed us from our bondage to Satan and his wiles. Furthermore, we have been redeemed from sin and its consequences, including fear, pain, negative feelings of inadequacy, depression, sorrow, and life of poverty and debt! We are now part of the Kingdom of God, and having been redeemed by the blood of Jesus, Satan cannot touch us.

Application:

For many people, though they confessed their sins and received their forgiveness, the root of sin is in them. A tree is truly dead only when its roots die. Otherwise, it always has a chance to spring back to life. In the same way, the root of sin remains in us unless it is eradicated. Thus when you whole-heartedly believe that Jesus paid all your debts by His blood, and when you confess His promise continuously that says, *"I am redeemed by the blood of Jesus and I belong to our Lord Jesus Christ"* the power in the blood of Christ is activated to render the root of sin powerless.

When I received this revelation from the Lord, I started declaring the redemptive power in the blood of Jesus. As I did this, it broke all the effects of sin in my life and gave me the confidence that I am a child of God and Satan has no authority over me.

Prayer:

Dear Lord, You are SO good to me. Thank You for Your precious blood that was shed two thousand years ago to atone all my sins. Satan cannot condemn me anymore, because you paid the penalty for all my sins. I am a child of the living God who was purchased—in FULL—by the blood of Jesus. Hallelujah! Thank You, Lord, for redeeming me by Your precious blood. I praise You that I am saved for all eternity. Satan has no power of any area of my life, because my life is Yours! In the redeeming name of our Savior, Lord Jesus Christ, I pray. Amen!

Reflection:

What are the eternal effects of Christ's atonement?

Can Satan have dominion over the people who have been redeemed by Jesus' blood?

Part Three

The Attributes

The Blood of Jesus forgives

"In Him we have redemption
through His blood, the forgiveness of sins,
according to the riches of His grace."

– Ephesians 1:7 (emphasis added)

Key Point:

The blood of Jesus has canceled all our wrongdoings.
There is no record—yes, there is nothing against us now!

Message:

The Creator of this entire universe has created each one
of us for a purpose. Ephesians 2:10 says, _"For we are his
workmanship, created in Christ Jesus for good works,"_ while Jeremiah 29:11 says, _"For I know the thoughts and plans that I
have for you, says the Lord . . ."_ (AMPC). These verses from
the Word of God confirm that God has a unique plan for
each of us.

Psalm 100:3 says, _"Know that the Lord, He is God; It is_

He who has made us and not we ourselves. We are His people and the sheep of His pasture." We belong to God because He has created us, and he has designated a purpose for each element of his creation.

Think for a moment about some of our modern creations. Designers have crafted certain machines to do certain things. Now, we know that cars are designed to run on roads. But, if a driver attempted to fly a car in the sky like an aircraft, the car would tear apart because "flying" is not the purpose for which the car was created. In the same way, if any of God's creation does things differently from what it was created to do, this could end up in the destruction of that creation.

When we do not fulfill our Creator's plan for which we were created, which is to glorify Him, we go against the purpose God has set for us. We thereby rebel against God and do not have right standing (righteousness) with God. Sin is an act of disobedience. The Greek word for sin is *"hamartia"* which means "missing the mark." People generally consider things like murder, adultery, stealing, lying and the like as the only sins. Of course, these are sins. But the Bible goes further and says, *"All unrighteousness is sin"* (1 John 5:17). When we go against the purposes of God and enter into unrighteousness, what else but God's forgiveness could bring us back into right standing with him?

While Jesus lived in this world, a paralytic man was brought to Him by the man's friends; *"When Jesus saw their faith, He said to the paralytic, 'Son, be of good cheer; your sins are forgiven you,'"* (Matthew 9:2).

Some of the scribes thought that it was blasphemy, because no one except God had the authority to forgive sins. Jesus, knowing their thoughts, said that they should know that the Son of Man has power on earth to forgive sins. He went on to say to the paralytic man, *"Arise, take up your bed and go to your house."* And the man arose and went to his house. The people marveled and glorified God for giving such power to men (Matthew 9:6-8).

God alone has the authority or ability to forgive sins. The same authority was given to the Son of Man. That is why Jesus could command the paralytic to walk. He demonstrated His authority.

God ordained that the forgiveness of sins could be obtained only by the sacrifice of sinless blood. Our righteous God, therefore, sent His only begotten Son, who is sinless, to shed His blood in order to forgive mankind's sins. Jesus said, *"This is my blood of the covenant, which is poured out for many for the forgiveness of sins"* (Mat-

We must never forget that this forgiveness was not cheap. It cost God the very life of His Son!

thew 26:28, NIV). Even today, when you believe that Jesus Christ is the Son of God who came down from heaven as a living sacrifice for your sins, when you confess your sins and repent of them, He will forgive all your sins (1 John 1:9). *We must never forget that this forgiveness was not cheap. It cost God the very life of His Son!*

The importance of the forgiveness of our sins is also

reflected in the Lord's Prayer. *"And forgive us our debts, as we forgive our debtors"* (Matthew 6:12); *"And forgive us our sins, for we also forgive everyone who is indebted to us"* (Luke 11:4).

Thus, Jesus relates forgiveness to the cancellation of debts.

When a person truly repents of his sins, the blood of Jesus will cancel out all his wrongdoings. When we repent and accept Christ, we are brought back into righteousness and back into our created purpose—to live in relationship with God.

In this context, I would like to share the story of a criminal who, having been washed by the blood of Jesus, died a happy death. This man was a hardcore criminal who had murdered many people and was sentenced to death. As the appointed time of his death approached, he was imprisoned in a dark cell. One day, a pastor who visited the prisoners, stood outside his cell and said, "Brother, Jesus loves you." This infuriated the prisoner who was awaiting his death. He yelled abusive things at the pastor and told him to go away. During his next visit, the pastor again told the prisoner, "My brother, Jesus loves you." This time the criminal, still using abusive language, spat on the pastor and threatened to harm him. When the pastor repeated the words, "Brother, Jesus loves you" for the third time during his next visit, the criminal burst out, "Hey! You don't know how many murders I have committed! Nobody can love me! No god can forgive my sins! You don't know anything about my past. You are grieving me by saying that Jesus loves me!"

The pastor looked at him tenderly and said, "A sinner like you was crucified on a cross along with Jesus. This man admitted that he was being punished justly for all his wrong doings, and repented of his sinful acts. As he was dying, he pleaded with Jesus to accept him into His kingdom. The same day, Jesus saved him and took him to Paradise (Luke 23:39-43). The same Jesus is compassionate, even today! He will never cast away anyone who comes to Him (John 6:37). Today, if you pray to Him, He will forgive all your sins, and when you die, He will take your soul to heaven."

The prisoner, though he was still facing death, was revived in his spirit on hearing this good news. He repented of his sins and accepted Jesus as his personal Savior. He began to read the Bible every day, and started to pray. Divine peace and joy filled his heart. On the day of his execution, he shaved, bathed, clothed himself, and walked majestically towards the place of his execution. There was joy radiating from his face. Everyone was amazed. "Look at the change that has come over a man who lived like a savage!" they exclaimed. What was the reason for this change? This prisoner had newfound faith that he would certainly go to heaven, as the blood of Jesus had forgiven all his sins. So, he could meet his physical death with a hopeful heart.

Application:

Yes, beloved! If you repent and confess your sins, the sacred blood of Jesus will bestow God's forgiveness upon you and restore you to your created purpose. Zechariah 13:1 says, *"On that day, there shall be a fountain opened for the house of David and the inhabitants of Jerusalem, to cleanse them from sin and uncleanness."* Christ's blood is that fountain that has been shed and stored up in the spirit realm. Upon confession and repentance, Christ's blood and God's forgiveness will come to you like the water that comes out a dam when its flood gate is opened. His blood removes all the sins you have ever committed and bestows God's forgiveness in your life.

Prayer:

Dear Father God, thank You, Lord for choosing me when I was in my mother's womb. You alone have the right to forgive our sins. I now confess all the sins that I have committed against You and others— sins by thought, word and deed. Jesus, by the precious blood that You shed for me, please forgive me and cancel all my wrongdoings. Help me restore the things I have taken from others. I accept You as the Lord and Savior of my life. In the forgiving name of our Savior, Lord Jesus Christ, I pray. Amen!

Reflection:

Can you write in a few words what 'forgiveness' means to you?

What did it cost God to forgive our sins?

What are the keys to receiving God's forgiveness for our sins?

The Blood of Jesus Cleanses Us

> *"The **blood of Jesus Christ His Son***
> ***cleanses us** from all sin."*
> — 1 John 1:7 (emphasis added)

Key Point:

The blood of Jesus cleanses, and will continue to cleanse us, from all the ill effects of sin so that we can have fellowship with God.

Message:

The Word of God says that the blood of Jesus Christ has the power not only to remove sins, but also to cleanse us from all sins.

We have already seen that forgiveness is a cancellation of all our wrongdoings. The records have been erased. But cleansing is different from forgiveness. We can find this explained in 1 John 1:9 (KJV): *"If we confess our sins,*

He is faithful and just to forgive us our sins and **to cleanse us from all unrighteousness"** (emphasis added). Jesus' blood cleanses us from all unrighteousness, which means it gives us a right standing with God by removing all unrighteousness in our lives.

In this sinful world, there are things that we accidentally, or sometimes even deliberately, see, hear, speak, touch, and think that have the potential to corrupt our lives. This affects our holy

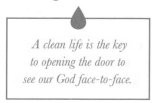

A clean life is the key to opening the door to see our God face-to-face.

walk with God. In order for God to abide in us, we must cleanse our eyes, ears, tongue, mind and body by applying the blood of Jesus *by faith* every day.

When we have continuous fellowship with God, the blood of Jesus will continuously cleanse us. It will help us to get rid of all the adverse effects of sins. Therefore, we must acknowledge that cleansing is an ongoing process that we need to actively pursue.

The Scripture tells us: *"Pursue . . . holiness, without which no one will see the Lord"* (Hebrews 12:14). In the Old Testament, we could see that the saints went through the ceremonial cleansing before getting involved with anything concerning God and His work (Exodus 30:17-21).

A clean life is the key to opening the door to see our God face to face.

Several years ago, a lady in our church shared her testimony—she had seen Jesus Christ! The following week, another member of the church testified that she, too, had seen Jesus. Hearing these testimonies filled me with a great longing to see Jesus face to face. I prayed earnestly, "Lord, I long to see You!"

One day as I was praying, I had a vision. I saw that Jesus was revealing Himself to many people. I cried out, "Lord, what is this? How is it that so many people are able to see You?" I then heard an audible voice from heaven saying, *"Blessed are the pure in heart; for they shall see God"* (Matthew 5:8).

It was then that I realized the importance of keeping my heart pure. Nothing is hidden from the sight of God. I began to confess all the sins that I had ever committed since my childhood. I reconciled with every person whose name God revealed to me. I started praying and asking God to cleanse my heart with the blood of Jesus. Finally, by the grace of God, the day dawned when I was able to see my Lord Jesus, face to face!

Application:

These days, there are many things that inject the poison of sin into our minds. As believers, we need to be careful to filter out the things that can seduce our mind and cater to the lust of the flesh.

However, there are situations and circumstances beyond our control. For example, we may catch a glimpse of posters or advertising signs that show people dressed seductively. These posters are often pasted all along the roads that we have to travel down. They seem quite unavoidable! The same is true of magazines and television ads. In public places, we may hear vulgar talk or music with inappropriate lyrics, and so on.

A preacher once said, "You cannot prevent the birds from flying over your head, but you can certainly keep them from building a nest in your hair."

In other words, temptations will surely "fly" our way. The devil will make sure of that. But if we are not careful to "keep them from building a nest" in our mind, the resulting sins may become Satan's stronghold in our life. As Romans 6:12-13 says, *"Therefore, do not let sin reign in your mortal body, that you should obey it in its lusts. And do not present your members as instruments of unrighteousness to sin, but present yourselves to God as being alive from the dead, and your members as instruments of righteousness to God."*

Our holy God wants to dwell in our hearts. Jesus said to his disciples, *"If anyone loves Me, he will keep My word; and My Father will love him, and We will come to him and make Our home with him,"* (John 14:23). If such a holy God desires to dwell in our hearts, should we not be doing everything possible to keep our hearts clean?

1 John 1:7 says, *"But if we [really] walk in the Light [that is, live each and every day in conformity with the precepts of God], as He Himself is in the Light, we have [true, unbroken] fellowship with one another [He with us, and we with Him], and the blood of Jesus His Son cleanses us from all sin [by erasing the stain of sin,* **keeping us cleansed from sin in all its forms and manifestations***]"* (AMP, emphasis added).

Reading this verse clearly reveals that when we have fellowship with God, and fellowship with children of God, and remain in constant contact with both, the blood of Jesus cleanses us of all our sins. Let us continuously cleanse our lives by the blood of Jesus so that we will be able to have the continuous presence of our God, the Creator of the universe, in our hearts. What a great joy it is to have ongoing fellowship with the Almighty God!

Prayer:

Dear Lord Jesus, I thank You for loving me so much that You shed Your blood to cleanse my sins. I repent for each and every sin that I have ever committed. Cleanse me inside out with Your precious blood. Help me guard what I choose to think, see, and hear. Keep me from the traps of carnality and my own flesh, from those who would seek to tempt me. Help me understand how holy You are and that we, too, must be holy. Come and live inside me. In the cleansing name of our Savior, Jesus Christ, I pray. Amen!

Reflection:

Why did the saints go through ceremonial cleansing before they could do anything for God?

Can you cleanse yourself of sins?

What are the benefits of cleansing by Jesus' blood in your life?

The Blood of Jesus Purges the Conscience

*"How much more shall **the blood of Christ,** who through the eternal Spirit offered Himself without spot to God, **cleanse your conscience** from dead works to serve the living God?"*

– Hebrews 9:14 (emphasis added)

Key Point:

The blood of Jesus not only cleanses us from sin, but also removes the guilt of past sin from our conscience, which Satan can try to use against us to prevent us from walking closely with our God.

Message:

When our daughter went to be with the Lord at the age of sixteen, I was heartbroken and crushed. In addition to this tragedy, many allegations and onslaughts on my family and our ministry followed that affected me deeply.

Deep in despair, I started to ponder whether these afflictions were a result of my past sins. Due to these thoughts of self-doubt, my mind was plagued for many months with guilt and shame. I am sure many of you, like me, may have gone through trying times in your life which have caused you to doubt the forgiveness of sins that we have received through the salvation extended by Christ. Perhaps, like the friends of Job, there have been people in your life who have made you question your righteousness—righteousness that was granted through the finished work of Christ on the cross—especially during times of adversity.

I have heard numerous testimonies of individuals who have been liberated from a life of extreme sin—such as murder, robbery, terrorism, etc. The one common thread that seems to bind such people together is a sense of guilt over their past actions. Oftentimes, when they are asked to testify about their newfound faith, or when they are asked to minister to others, they shy away because of their past. They continue to be riddled with a sense of remorse, and their guilt pricks them. Especially when things go wrong in life and circumstances are negative, they presume they are being punished for past sins. It takes them a long time to come to grips with the fact that their sins have been completely cleansed and totally eradicated by the blood of Christ.

King David experienced the grief of a guilty conscience. 1 Chronicles 21:1 says, *"Satan rose up against Israel and incited David to take a census of Israel"* (NIV). This was written right after a great victory over the Philistines, so the sin was probably related to a problem with pride and self-reliance. It seems, therefore, that David's intent was to increase the royal power in a way that contrasted with humble reliance on God. The Lord was displeased with the census. Soon after, when the numbers were presented to the King, a plague started among the Israelites. The Bible records that nearly 70,000 people died as a result of this plague. When David saw the hand of the Lord against his people as a result of his own disobedience and sin, his conscience was disturbed. So, David prayed to the Lord saying, *"I have sinned; I, the shepherd, have done wrong. These are but sheep. What have they done? Let your hand fall on me and my family"* (2 Samuel 24:17, NIV). Like David who stood in the gap and pleaded with the Lord on behalf of his people, the divine High Priest, our Lord Jesus Christ, stands in the gap and makes petition for us. But where David pleaded because of his own guilt, Jesus, who was guiltless, pleads on our behalf because of our own guilt.

The Bible says in Hebrews 4:15, *"For we do not have a high priest who is unable to empathize with our weaknesses, but we have one who has been tempted in every way, just as we are—yet he did not sin"* (NIV). This means that Jesus understands our feelings of guilt and shame, which are brought on by the Devil.

It says in 1 John 1:7, *"The blood of Jesus Christ His Son cleanses (removes) us from all sin and guilt [keeps us cleansed from sin in all its forms and manifestations]"* (AMPC). This means that no matter how great or small our sins are, they are washed clean and are remembered no longer!

Jesus' blood not only removes our sin but also cleanses our guilty conscience, which often is the result of sin. This means that every sin we have ever committed has been expunged, and thus, cannot affect our future in any way.

Isaiah 1:18-19 says, "*'Come now, and let us reason together,' Says the LORD, 'Though your sins are like scarlet, They shall be as white as snow; Though they are red like crimson, They shall be as wool. If you are willing and obedient, You shall eat the good of the land.'*" Isaiah the prophet points out that willful obedience to accept the Word of God will yield the fruit of a pure conscience.

Prior to his conversion, Paul the apostle was a persecutor of the churches. In particular, the Bible clearly says that he gave his approval to the death of Stephen (Acts 8:1). After his conversion experience on the road to Damascus, his conscience was surely grieved concerning the death of Stephen and many others who had been persecuted by him. This is why he writes that he wishes to "forget" his past and anticipate his future (Philippians 3:13). This doesn't mean his memory was erased or that the past had somehow been re-written. It only means that Paul was free of any guilt that he may have felt from his past actions because he believed in the power of the blood of Christ to

> *Jesus' blood not only removes our sin but also cleanses our guilty conscience, which often is the result of sin. This means that every sin we have ever committed has been expunged, and thus, cannot affect our future in any way.*

purify the conscience. This attitude enabled him to live in the present and fulfill God's call in his life. In Philippians 3:14, Paul says *"I press on towards the goal for the prize of the upward call of God in Christ Jesus"* (NASB).

In Isaiah 53:10 we read, *"Yet it pleased the LORD to bruise Him; He has put Him to grief. When You make His soul an offering for sin, He shall see His seed, He shall prolong His days, And the pleasure of the LORD shall prosper in His hand."* The Hebrew word for "an offering for sin" is 'asham', meaning '(as) a guilt offering.'[2] Hence, Jesus' atoning sacrifice on the cross has fulfilled all God's requirements of guilt offering. Jesus' blood alone has the power to purge our conscience so that we may serve the living God. An unblemished conscience is an absolute necessity to further our relationship with God.

Application:

Even after we are cleansed by the blood of Jesus, we often still sin, both knowingly and unknowingly. Instead of being discouraged by a guilty conscience when we do so, we must appropriate the finished work of Jesus on the cross. We should claim the blood of Christ again, and the power of His blood will continue to cleanse us from guilt and sin.

Beloved child of God, Satan brings to recollection our past sins, and tries to deter us from the race set before us by God. But the Bible says that the Lord blots out our transgressions and sins, and remembers them no longer (Isaiah 43:25; Hebrews 8:12).

Isaiah 53:5 says, *"But He was wounded for our transgres-*

sions, *He was bruised for our guilt and iniquities; the chastisement [needful to obtain] peace and well-being for us was upon Him, and with the stripes [that wounded] Him we are healed and made whole"* (AMPC). This means that every physical wound that drew blood from His body was inflicted on Him so that we might attain peace and healing. This includes healing for the wounds in our inner man, which are caused by a marred conscience. The word for peace used here in this passage is "shalom" which means "wholeness" or "completeness."[3] The blood of Jesus alone can grant this healing, purge our conscience, and bestow peace, which the world can never give.

Prayer:

Our Loving Heavenly Father, how thankful are we that You are the God of forgiveness. You not only cleanse us of our sins, but you also wipe every record of our sins from Your memory. You sent Your Son, whom You love so dearly, to suffer and die on the cross to erase our sins. Thank you for cleansing me of my sin. I pray that even as I call on the blood of Jesus to wash me from within, that You will heal not just my physical body, but also wipe clean my guilt-ridden conscience that prevents me from coming boldly into Your presence. I know that my past does not matter because You have made it as white as snow. Thank You that I can approach Your Throne of Mercy and have my sins and my conscience purged. In the merciful name of my Lord Jesus Christ, I pray. Amen!

Reflection:

What are the effects or consequences of guilt that you have experienced in your life?

How can you overcome guilt in your life?

The Blood of Jesus Sanctifies

> *"Therefore, Jesus also, that He might **sanctify the people with His own blood,** suffered outside the gate."*

— Hebrews 13:12 (emphasis added)

Key Point:

Total submission to our Lord enables the blood of Jesus to sanctify us and bring us to a place of communion with God. In this place, the wonders and miracles of God flow in and through our lives, and we can live a supernatural life that brings glory to Him.

Message:

To the casual reader, it may appear that there is little difference between cleansing and sanctification. But there is a great and important difference.

According to Bakers Evangelical Dictionary, the

generic meaning of sanctification is "the state of proper functioning." To sanctify someone or something is to set that person or thing apart for the use intended by its designer. The Greek word sanctification, "hagiasmos" is translated as "holiness." To sanctify, therefore, means "to make holy."[4]

In the Old Testament, entering God's presence was only possible for sanctified priests. God asked Moses to build the tabernacle according to the model in heaven (Exodus 25:40; Hebrews 8:5). In this tabernacle, there were three places: the outer court, inner court, and the most Holy Place. A high priest would have to pass through the outer and inner courts in order to reach the most Holy Place. God promised to speak to the priest when he reached the Holy of Holies (Exodus 25:22). It was a step-by-step process laid out by God, allowing the priests to meet Him in the Holy Place.

In the same way, I believe that a person must go through a step-by-step process in order to come to that place of sanctification. First, a person's sins must be removed. Cleansing follows this, and that leads to sanctification. In other words, removal and cleansing of sin precedes sanctification.

In his letters, the apostle Paul has clearly distinguished this process: *"Therefore if anyone cleanses himself from the latter, he will be a vessel for honor, sanctified and useful for the Master, prepared for every good work"* (2 Timothy 2:21). Ephesians 5:26 says, *"That he might sanctify it, having cleansed it by the washing of water with the Word"* (ASV). Removing and cleansing of sin have mostly to do with the old life. Sanctification, however, concerns the new life, the characteristics of which must be imparted by God. Sanctification, which brings union with God, is the peculiar fullness of blessing purchased for us by the blood of Jesus.

In serving God, the priests were required to be sanctified (consecrated), whereas the Levites, who served a supporting role to the priests, just needed to be cleansed. This is because only the priests had to enter into the presence of God in the Holy Place and the High Priest to the most Holy of Holies (Hebrews 9:6-7). From this we can infer that a person must be sanctified in order to become intimate with God. As a result, God is able to speak to him and through him to others. *The sanctified believer becomes a powerful instrument in the hands of God.*

God sanctified His people so that He could dwell among them. Exodus 29:44-46 says, *"And I will sanctify the Tent of Meeting and the altar; I will sanctify also both Aaron and his sons to minister to Me in the priest's office. And I will dwell among the Israelites and be their God. And they shall know [from personal experience] that I am the Lord their God, Who brought them forth out of the land of Egypt that I might dwell among them; I am the Lord their God"* (AMP).

The children of the Israelites were greatly blessed due to sanctification. They witnessed nature give way supernaturally to God's power, and because they were sanctified to God, their enemies were crushed.

In the Old Testament, God required the people to follow elaborate rituals. This included sprinkling and applying the blood of animal sacrifices in order to be sanctified. But in the New Testament, by the grace of God, the blood of Jesus sanctifies a person (Hebrew 13:12). Now, we don't need to enter the Most Holy Place because the Holy Spirit lives inside us and sanctifies us.

Apart from the blood of Christ, we also see in the Bible that God uses His Word (John 17:17) and His Spirit (1 Peter 1:2; 2 Thessalonians 2:13) to sanctify us. Human beings cannot sanctify themselves. It is God, and only God, who sanctifies (1 Corinthians 1:30, 6:11). Though the Word of God says that we have already been sanctified, I strongly believe that we need to participate in the life-long process of sanctification

Even Jesus, who was born without sin, said *"And for their sakes I sanctify Myself . . ."* (John 17:19).

Jesus did not say, "I sanctified." Rather, He uses the present tense "sanctify." This shows us that Jesus totally yielded Himself every day to God's will, and in doing so, He was able to clearly reflect God to the people in the world. In order to come to the place of sanctification, we must overcome temptation, and submit as a servant to God to fulfill the calling in our lives.

Application:

When a believer overcomes temptation, the Lord, through His blood, places him or her at the highest level of holiness, or sanctification. "Holiness" in us is nothing short of oneness with God. Once we come to that place of sanctification, miracles will begin to flow, as was the case with the Israelites.

I have observed that every time I need to preach the Word of God, some pressing social, domestic or even ministry-related work comes my way. This seemingly urgent work comes just in time to eat into my personal time with the Lord. But I try to get these tasks taken care of by someone else, or even ignore them when possible, and I wait in the presence of God. I ask God to cleanse and sanctify me so that I may be a useful vessel in His hands. When I prioritize spending time in His presence, I can be sure that the mighty presence of God will be there each time I minister.

It is purely by grace that the Almighty God has chosen to abide in us and work through us. He chooses to use us to reveal His love and power to the people of this world. If you desire to be mightily used by our Lord, ask Him regularly to cleanse and sanctify you by His blood.

1 Peter 2:9 says, *"But you are a chosen generation, a royal priesthood, a holy nation, His own special people, that you may proclaim the praises of Him who called you out of darkness into His marvelous light."*

Prayer:

Dear God, I thank You for choosing to have an intimate relationship with me. I declare that I am redeemed by Your blood. Lord, I sometimes struggle to defeat certain sins in my life. Give me the strength to overcome all temptations and break any strongholds that Satan may

have in my life, so that I may come to the place of sanctification.
Wash me once more. Commune with me and guide me. Help me to
become a vessel of honor, and use me as an instrument in Your hands.
In the sanctifying name of my Lord Jesus Christ, I pray. Amen!

Reflection:

Is sanctification a lifelong process?

What are the reasons sanctification is necessary and how
can we attain sanctification in our lives?

The Blood of Jesus Removes All Barriers

*"Not with the blood of goats and calves, but **with His own blood He entered the Most Holy Place** once for all, having obtained eternal redemption."*

– Hebrews 9:12 (emphasis added)

Key Point:

The blood of Jesus can remove all the physical and spiritual barriers that hinder God's blessings meant for us. All we have to do is call upon His blood in faith, and God's blessings are for us!

Message:

Today, people have many barriers in their lives. There could be barriers in finding a spouse or in conceiving a baby. There could be barriers in finding the right job, in receiving a promotion, constructing a home, or in building a business. There are even barriers in the lives of children. And, more importantly, there are barriers to receiving the blessings of God.

The blood of Jesus not only removes the stain of sin within us, it also removes any barriers that sin establishes between God and us. Isaiah 59:1-2 tells us that our iniquities separate us from God, standing as barriers that block blessings from God, as He cannot hear our prayers: *"Behold, the Lord's hand is not shortened that it cannot save, nor his ear heavy that it cannot hear. But your iniquities have separated you from your God and your sins have hidden His face from you, so that He will not hear."*

Once, while ministering in a foreign country, I visited the home of a man who was a very rich and highly respected person in society. Christian meetings were held in his home every week. He also supported pastors who came to preach the Word of God. However, there came a time when this rich man faced heavy losses in his business. The situation was so bad that the bank was going to auction everything he owned. When I prayed for him, I was made aware of his sinful life. This is what was blocking the flow of God's blessings into his life.

Today, like this rich man, many people seek the blessings of God while they continue in their sinful lifestyle. Proverbs 28:9 clearly says, *"One who turns away his ear from hearing the law, even his prayer is an abomination."* We cannot hide anything from God. *". . . But all things are naked and open to the eyes of Him to whom we* must give *account"* (Hebrews 4:13).

If a person continues to live in sin, God cannot hear his prayers or bail him out of his problems. If a person truly repents and seeks the power of the blood of Jesus, then God will hear his prayers. The Bible says, *"O You who hear prayer, to You all flesh will come"* (Psalm 65:2).

The blood has the power to remove sin barriers!

We discover from the Bible that Daniel, a faithful servant of God, was fasting and praying but had not seen any results. The answer to Daniel's prayer was delayed by twenty-one days because the Prince of the kingdom of Persia resisted God's messenger angel. We are told that Michael, one of the chief princes, was sent to help the messenger angel, resulting in Daniel receiving the answer to his prayer (Daniel 10:12-13).

According to the Word of God, there are three heavens. The first heaven is the firmament or atmosphere surrounding the earth, which God spoke into existence on

The blood has the power to remove sin barriers!

the second day of creation (Genesis 1:6-8). The second heaven is the high places where principalities, powers, rulers of darkness and spiritual wickedness dwell (Ephesians 6:12). The third heaven is where God dwells (2 Corinthians 12:1-6).

Satan, the master of sin and ruler of this world (John 14:30), establishes spiritual barriers in the second heaven in order to block our blessings. This is why Daniel could not receive the answer to his prayer for twenty-one days.

Satan is a spirit who fights against us in the spiritual realm day and night, in various ways. Satan places barriers in the spiritual realm so we don't receive spiritual blessings in our life. But Jesus Christ came into this world not only to save sinners, but also to destroy Satan and his works.

- *"Inasmuch then as the children have partaken of flesh and blood, He Himself likewise shared in the same, that through death He might destroy him who had the power of death, that is, the devil"* (Hebrews 2:14).
- *" . . . For this purpose the Son of God was manifested, that he might destroy the works of the devil"* (1 John 3:8).

A wonderful lady who was a partner of our ministry was having difficulty entering into a business contract with a very prominent company. One day, she heard my teachings on the blood of Jesus. She was so excited to learn about all the blessings available through His blood, that she applied the blood of Jesus and prayed over her client. Shortly after this, the person inside the organization who was hindering her contract was fired from his job. Jesus' blood breaks down barriers!

After His death, burial and resurrection, Jesus took the blood, which He shed in this world, to the most Holy Place in heaven, the third heaven (Hebrews 9:12, 24). When this happened, the blood of Jesus tore down and completely removed the spiritual barriers established by Satan in the second heaven. As written in Micah 2:13, the One who breaks barriers broke all the barriers in our lives! No longer could Satan hinder God's answers to our prayers. Now we have an "open heaven" over our lives. The blood of Jesus opened a way into the third heaven. If the blood of Jesus removed spiritual barriers in the heavenly realms then, will it not remove all the barriers in your life today? The blood will never lose its power. It definitely will work the same, even today!

Application:

Yes, when you apply the blood of Jesus over a situation, the barriers have no option but to go! Sin barriers, whether created by your sin or the sin of someone else, can seem impossible to overcome. And they can't be overcome on your own, but when the blood of Jesus is applied to the situation, all sin barriers are removed.

Prayer:

Dear Heavenly Father who loves me much, thank You for removing all spiritual barriers by the blood of Your Son Jesus. I believe that Your precious blood is able to remove all the barriers in my life which are delaying my promotion, marriage or the gift of children. I know You can remove barriers that are affecting the education of my children, my health, my peace of mind, employment, family life, job, and every other problem in my life. Thank You, Lord, for removing these barriers so that I may inherit the blessings You have prepared for me. In the matchless name of Jesus, I pray. Amen!

Reflection:

What are the barriers that hinder God's blessings in your life?

How did Jesus break these barriers and what is the impact of it now?

Part four

The Blessings

The Blood of Jesus Gives Victory

*"And **they overcame him by the blood of the Lamb**…"*

– Revelation 12:11 (emphasis added)

Key Point:

The blood of Jesus has already given us victory over all our problems—we just have to claim it! Our enemies will not defeat us. We are not victims but victors over all our circumstances because of the blood of Jesus working in our life.

Message:

During my childhood, my grandmother often told me, "You'll be victorious if you say 'Victory in the blood of Jesus.'" Every time I wrote an exam, I used to declare this seemingly "magic" phrase while answering the questions.

I always passed with flying colors. Whenever I faced problems in life, I made it a habit to say, "Victory in the blood of Jesus." I still use the same words, but I say it with even more conviction and faith, because I have seen the power of this phrase throughout my life.

While Jesus was in human form, He faced trials, temptations, problems, enemies, the powers of this world and much more. After spending forty days and nights in the desert without food, Jesus was hungry. The tempter came to Him and said, *"If You are the Son of God, command this stone to become bread"* (Luke 4:3). This temptation was in relation to the lust of the flesh.

"Then, the devil took Jesus to a very high mountain and **showed Him** *all the kingdoms of the world in all their splendor, and said to Him, 'All this authority I will give You, and their glory; for this has been delivered to me, and I give it to whomever I wish. Therefore, if You will worship before me, all will be Yours'"* (Luke 4:6-7, emphasis added). Now, this temptation was in relation to the lust of the eyes.

Finally, the devil took Him to Jerusalem and set Him on the highest point of the temple. The devil said to Him, *"If You are the Son of God, throw Yourself down from here. For it is written: 'He shall give His angels charge over You, to keep You' and, 'In their hands they shall bear you up, lest you dash your foot against a stone,'"* (Luke 4:9-11). This temptation was to do with the pride of life.

In all these temptations, Jesus was victorious, not just over Satan, but also over the lust of flesh, the lust of eyes, and the pride of life. 1 John 2:16 says, *"For all that is in the world—the lust of the flesh, the lust of the eyes, and the pride of life—is not of the Father but is of the world." Jesus not only overcame the devil and his temptations, but also overcame all other earthly problems—victoriously!*

The world system and the devil have promoted a false sense of power so that people are unable to see that all power belongs to our God (1 Chronicles 29:11). Many think that money is power. People are slaves to money. It controls them. On one occasion, Jesus was asked to pay tax. Even though He had no money, He was not anxious at all. He simply asked Peter to catch a fish, take a silver coin from its mouth and pay the tax for Him and also for His disciples (Matthew 17:24-27). Thus, Jesus had victory in financial situations!

> *Jesus not only overcame the devil and his temptations, but also overcame all other earthly problems—victoriously!*

The Pharisees once wanted to trap Jesus by asking, *"Is it lawful to pay taxes to the Roman Emperor, or not?"* He told them to pay Caesar what was due to Caesar and to God what was due to God. Likewise, He answered all the clever questions of His enemies with such wisdom that nobody dared to ask Him anything after that (Matthew 22:46). Thus, he triumphed over all His crafty cunning enemies in this world.

In the garden of Gethsemane, He surrendered himself completely to the will of the Father by saying, *"Father, if it is Your will, take this cup away from Me; nevertheless not My will, but Yours, be done"* (Luke 22:42). Here we can see that Jesus was victorious even over His own will!

When Pilate told Jesus that he had authority to set Him free, or to have Him crucified, Jesus showed no fear in the face of Pilate's authority. He answered, *"You could have no power at all against Me unless it had been given you from above . . ."* (John 19:11). Thus, Jesus Christ overcame the threatening power of the worldly authorities.

Jesus was whipped and was crowned with thorns. His body bled profusely. He was laid on the cross, and his hands and legs were nailed to the cross. Undergoing enormous physical suffering, He finally gave up his life saying, *"It is finished"* (John 19:30). By submitting Himself to all this brutality and terrible suffering, Jesus gained victory over all physical suffering.

1 Corinthians 15:26 tells us that by dying on the cross and rising from the grave on the third day, Jesus conquered His final enemy—death!

Jesus remained focused on what He was to accomplish in this world. His faith did not waver, no matter how hungry He was. He did not go ahead of God's timing. He was in tune with God's will, even during testing times or trials. He chose to remain steadfast and be true to the Father. He was confident that He could overcome the devil's wiles as He stood upon the solid promises of God the Father.

Thus, Jesus Christ, who triumphantly overcame all temptations, trials and tribulations says, *"In the world you have tribulation* and *trials* and *distress* and *frustration; but be of good cheer [take courage; be confident, certain, undaunted]! For I have overcome the world. [I have deprived it of power to harm you and have conquered it for you]"* (John 16:33, AMPC).

The One who overcame the world is the One who gives us victory today!

- *"But thanks be to God who gives us the victory through our Lord Jesus Christ"* (1 Corinthians 15:57).
- *"Now thanks be to God who always leads us in triumph in Christ"* (2 Corinthians 2:14).
- *"Yet in all these things we are more than conquerors through Him who loved us"* (Romans 8:37).

The same blood of Jesus flows through our veins, and so, we too can lead victorious lives. Let us inherit the victory earned by Jesus through His blood. Then we too can certainly overcome the devil and his wiles, the tribulations of this world, our self-will, the threatening dominance of the worldly authorities, physical sufferings, and even the fear of death!

Application:

Proverbs 18:21 says, *"Death and life are in the power of the tongue, and those who love it will eat its fruit."* Accordingly, whatever you confess with your tongue will definitely manifest in your life. When you believe wholeheartedly that the blood of Jesus gives you victory, you should declare that *there is victory in the blood of Jesus*—every minute of each day. This continuous confession will help you overcome the devil and his wicked plans to bring ruin into your life and into the world.

So, what are you waiting for? Jesus doesn't necessarily need to make you find silver coins in the mouth of a fish, but you can certainly expect that He will help you have victory over all your problems by the power of His blood. Whatever His mode of operation, you too can join the host of believers around the world who have testified to the validity of the truth about the blood of Jesus in their lives. Victory is already yours! Claim it now!

Today, you may be struggling against the devil and his deceitful plans. You may be fighting the world with its corrupt attractions. You may be wondering if you can ever overcome them. However, the verses above clearly assure us that it is possible to overcome all these things by the blood of Jesus. We can lead a victorious life because God's Word is never wrong.

Prayer:

Dear God Almighty, Your Son shed His blood for us to lead a victorious life! Oh Lord, take away all the failures in my life and help me lead a successful life. Give me victory in my studies, in my ministry, in my business, in my family life, over the wiles of the devil and even over my fear of death. Help me to face all problems and struggles boldly by Your grace. I believe and I proclaim that there is victory in the blood of Jesus. I am more than a conqueror through Him who loves me. Thank you, Lord for the victory! In the victorious name of our Lord, Jesus Christ, I pray. Amen!

Reflection:

What are the tools necessary to inherit Jesus' victory in your life?

Why does God require us to celebrate even before the victory comes?

The Blood of Jesus Grants Peace

*"Having made **peace through the blood** of His cross."*

– Colossians 1:20 (emphasis added)

Key Point:

The blood of Jesus has given us peace in our heart, peace in the midst of all our problems, and peace between our God and us. Praise Jesus for the amazing gift of peace through His blood!

Message:

We know our Lord Jesus Christ came into this world to give peace in our mind, joy to our spirit, healing to our body and eternal life to our soul. Let us meditate on how the blood of Jesus grants us peace in every area of life.

Peace in the Heart

Jesus Christ is the only one who can give peace to all of us. The Bible says, *"Surely he hath borne our **griefs**, and carried our **sorrows**: yet we did esteem him stricken, smitten of God, and afflicted. But He was wounded for our transgressions, He was bruised for our iniquities; the chastisement for our peace was upon Him, and by His stripes we are healed"* (Isaiah 53:4-5, emphasis added).

To bring peace to mankind, our Lord Jesus Christ took all our griefs, sorrows and the punishment for all our sins upon Himself. The Hebrew word for grief is "choli" which means "affliction, disease, and griefs."[5] The Hebrew word for sorrows is "makob" which means "pain, sorrow, and sufferings."[6] In short, Jesus has carried all our troubles and as an exchange through His blood He has given His peace to us. Therefore, His holy blood alone can bring real peace into our hearts.

When a person realizes his sins, confesses them to the Lord Jesus Christ, asks for His forgiveness, and accepts Him as his personal Savior, the first transformation that takes place within him is a feeling of immense peace. How does this happen? The blood of Jesus washes away the sins that convict him.

This is a spiritual cleansing experienced by faith leading to divine peace.

This is precisely what happened when I committed my life to Jesus Christ. The blood of Jesus cleansed me of all my sins, and the peace of God entered my heart. Like me, all who truly receive Jesus into their hearts experience divine peace in their heart.

Peace in the Midst of Turbulence

Once, when Jesus was on a boat with his disciples, there was a storm. The boat was tossed about by the waves and was about to sink. Panicked, the disciples woke Jesus up and said, "Teacher, do you not care that we are perishing?" Jesus got up and rebuked the winds and commanded the waves to stop. He said, "*Peace, be still . . .*" (Mark 4:39). Immediately the sea became calm. Matthew 12:34 says, "*out of the abundance of the heart, the mouth speaks.*" Here we can see that even in the midst of a natural calamity beyond human control, Jesus was able to release the word "peace." This is because, even as a man, he had peace within Himself. It was the peace within Him that gave Him the authority to command the calm.

In another instance, Jesus wanted to feed people who had come to hear His sermon. There were about five thousand men, besides women and children. When Jesus asked His disciples to feed the multitude, they told Him, "*There is a lad here who has five barley loaves and two small fish, but what are they among so many?*" (John 6:9). Though they spoke words of inadequacy to Jesus, He was not worried. Jesus had peace within Himself. Jesus blessed the loaves and fish and fed all the people. The remaining fragments were gathered in twelve baskets! He was able to perform this miracle because of the peace within Himself.

Judas Iscariot was with Jesus for about three and a

half years. He had seen the glory and power of Jesus. But he betrayed Jesus for thirty silver coins. This terrible situation did not affect Jesus because of the peace within Himself. Jesus Christ could even address Judas as "My friend" (Matthew 26:50, NLT). Jesus was peaceful even when His own disciple betrayed Him.

Jesus was whipped, His flesh torn, and His hands and feet nailed to the cross. Amidst such terrible suffering, Jesus was able to pray, *"Father, forgive them for they know not what they do"* (Luke 23:34). Even when He was about to die, Jesus had divine peace.

In the midst of situations like these—storms, challenges, betrayal, and even when he was crucified—Jesus had peace within Himself. The Bible says that He is the Prince of Peace (Isaiah 9:6), meaning He is the only source of peace. It is this peace that He promises to give each one of us.

John 14:27 says, *"Peace I leave with you, My peace I give to you; not as the world gives do I give to you. Let not your heart be troubled, neither let it be afraid."* Yes, it is the blood of Jesus alone that can bring real peace into our troubled lives.

Peace with God

Once, the children of Israel did evil and the Lord delivered them into the hands of their enemies. When the Israelites planted their crops, the Midianites, Amalekites and other Eastern peoples invaded the country and ruined the crops. They took every living thing—sheep, cattle, donkeys, etc. Because the powerful Midianites were so oppressive, the Israelites prepared shelters for themselves in mountain clefts, caves, and strongholds. Under these circumstances, they cried out to the Lord for help.

The Angel of the Lord appeared to Gideon and assured him that God was with him. When Gideon asked for proof, God revealed His name as **Jehovah Shalom,** the God of peace. In doing so, the Lord implied that He now made peace with His chosen ones. This gave Gideon the confidence to fight the enemy. With an army of just 300, they overcame their enemies (Judges 6 & 7). When God is with us who can be against us?

When God created Adam and Eve, He had close fellowship with them. God had the same fellowship with His chosen people, as we see in the lives of holy men like Enoch, Noah, Abraham and David. But when mankind sinned, sin drove a wedge into the relationship between man and God. Sin brought enmity with God.

James 4:4 says, *"Adulterers and adulteresses! Do you not know that friendship with the world is enmity with God? Whoever therefore wants to be a friend of the world makes himself an enemy of God."*

Romans 8:7 says, *"Because the carnal mind is enmity against God . . ."*

However, Ephesians 2:13-16 says, *"But now in Christ Jesus you who once were far off have been brought near by the blood of Christ. For He Himself is our peace, who has made both one, and has broken down the middle wall of separation, having abolished in His flesh the enmity,* that is, *the law of commandments* contained *in ordinances, so as to create in Himself one new man* from *the two,* thus *making peace, and that He might reconcile them both to God in*

The blood of Christ takes away all enmity between God and us!

one body through the cross, thereby putting to death the enmity."

Colossians 1:19-21 states, *"For it pleased the Father that in Him all the fullness should dwell, and by Him to reconcile all things to Himself, by Him, whether things on earth or things in heaven, having made peace through the blood of His cross. And you, who once were alienated and enemies in your mind by wicked works, yet now He has reconciled."*

The blood of Christ takes away all enmity between God and us!

Jesus Christ has brought reconciliation through His blood, re-establishing peace with God. What a great blessing!

We see that the blood of Jesus gives peace in our hearts, grants peace in troubled times, and brings peace with God through reconciliation.

Application:

Trust Him and go after the peace of God by reading the scriptures and allowing the fruits of the Holy Spirit to manifest in your life (Psalm 119:165; Galatians 5:22). These practices and spiritual disciplines will help you to sustain the peace of God that was bestowed in your life by the blood of Jesus.

Isaiah 26:3 says, *"You will keep him in perfect peace, whose mind is stayed on You because he trusts in You."* May this precious blood of Jesus, which was shed for us, keep your hearts and minds in peace forever!

Prayer:

Dear Heavenly Father, I thank You for Your Son, Jesus, who shed His precious blood to bring peace into my life. In the midst of suffering, I will seek You with all my heart. Be gracious to me. I thank you, Jesus, for reconciling me with my God through Your blood. As Your Word declares, let Your peace and happiness reign in my life, and in my home, now and forever. In the sweet name of Jesus Christ, the Prince of Peace, I pray. Amen!

Reflection:

Write the reasons why you do not have peace in your life.

How can you seize the peace of Jesus in your life? How do you stay in that peace bestowed by Jesus' blood?

The Blood of Jesus Redeems Us from Curses

*"Then Noah built an altar to the Lord, and took of every clean animal and of every clean bird, and **offered burnt offerings on the altar**. And the Lord smelled a soothing aroma. Then the Lord said in His heart, '**I will never again curse the ground for man's sake,** although the imagination of man's heart is evil from his youth; nor will I again destroy every living thing as I have done.'"*

– Genesis 8:20-21 (emphasis added)

Key Point:

The blood of Jesus has removed all our curses. Nothing we have said or done, neither anything our family has said or done, can bring a curse into our lives! All curses have no more consequence in our life because we have applied the blood of Christ over our families and over ourselves. We are a blessed people!

Message:

There once lived a very rich landlord. He was a wicked and cruel man. He had committed many murders, robbed people and destroyed many lives. One day, I met the grandson of one of this man's many "agents." He said to

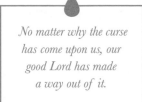

No matter why the curse has come upon us, our good Lord has made a way out of it.

me, "My grandparents were cohorts of that landlord's family. Because of the things they did all those years ago, the curses of all those they hurt are now upon us. We have accepted Jesus as our personal Savior and we are His children now; yet there are many painful things in our family. We are sure that all this is due to the crimes of our forefathers and the curses they brought upon us."

Is there redemption from such curses? Before we meditate upon the biblical solution to all curses, let us understand their source.

The devil tempted the first parents to sin against God. He led them to eat the fruit of the forbidden tree. Since they had gone against the command of God, God laid curses on them. Since then, man has continued to bring curses upon himself and his descendants in many different ways. *No matter why the curse has come upon us, our good Lord has made a way out of it.*

We see from the first two chapters of Genesis that everything God created was good and blessed—not cursed. Curse was a result of sin. Sin was introduced to the world by the serpent.

The first curse that was pronounced was on the serpent: *"Because you have done this, you are cursed more than all the cattle, and more than every beast of the field. On your belly you shall go, and you shall eat dust, all the days of your life"* (Genesis 3:14). I believe that since Satan was the first recipient of the curse, He became the author of the curses. Moreover, he is the ruler of the world, and he has the authority to bring the curses on his subjects.

But praise the Lord, for Satan's authority and power were totally dismantled by our Lord Jesus on the cross (Colossians 2:14-15; Hebrews 2:14; 1 John 3:8). Jesus' blood that was shed, especially from the heel when the Roman soldiers pierced His leg with the nails, bruised the head of Satan (Genesis 3:14-15).

We see examples of the power of speaking blessings and curses in the Old Testament. In the book of Numbers, Balak, the king of Moab, is frightened by reports of the approaching Israelites. He decides to hire Balaam to pronounce curses upon Israel so that he will be able to defeat them in war. Even though King Balak of Moab offered money to Balaam, to Balak's great surprise, Balaam uttered blessings for Israel instead of curses (Numbers 22–24).

In Genesis, when Noah came out of the ark, the first thing he did was build an altar. He then sacrificed a clean animal unto the Lord. When the blood of the sacrificial animal was shed onto the earth, the Lord made a covenant for all mankind. He said that He would not curse the ground because of the sin of man.

We are blessed by the Almighty God. Satan cannot curse what the Lord has blessed! *If an animal's blood could remove such a great curse, what great deliverance is in the powerful blood of the spotless Lamb of God, Jesus Christ!*

We can take comfort in reading this verse: ***"Christ has redeemed us from the curse of the Law***, *having become a curse for us (for it is written cursed is everyone who hangs on a tree)"* (Galatians 3:13, emphasis added). Praise God for all He has done for us!

We can have the assurance that Jesus has taken all our curses upon Himself! The moment we proclaim the power of His blood, we are instantly redeemed from all curses.

Application:

Ask the Lord to show you the hidden areas of sin through which the devil has a hold in your lives. Ask God's forgiveness for your sins, as well as the sins of your forefathers. Besides this, you must also cancel the devil's right to execute the curses in your lives. When we apply the blood of Jesus by faith, His blood has the power to nullify all curses and bring great blessing into our lives!

Prayer:

Dear Lord, thank You for making a provision to remove all curses from the lives of Your people. Please look upon my life, bogged down by curses. Lord Jesus, I believe with all my heart that Your precious blood alone can remove all curses from my life. I ask You, Lord to eliminate all curses from my family, my business, my ministry and all the works of my hands. I know that You will turn the curses into blessings! In the curse-breaking name of our Savior, Jesus Christ, I pray. Amen!

Reflection:

What are the ways that curses can come upon your life?

If the Lord has blessed you, Satan cannot curse you! If that is so, how could the curse have an effect on you now?

The Blood of Jesus Protects

*"Now **the blood shall be a sign for you on the houses** where you are. And when I see the blood, I will pass over you; and **the plague shall not be on you to destroy you** when I strike the land of Egypt."*

— Exodus 12:13 (emphasis added)

Key Point:

The blood of Jesus is the hedge and the protection for our families, our substance, our work, and us. As long as we stay under His blood, we are safe from Satan—physically, as well as spiritually. No enemy can touch our bodies or our souls!

Message:

We read in the book of Job that Satan could not touch Job, as God had put a hedge around him, his family, surroundings (neighborhood), business, and substance. Satan asks God, *"Have You not made a hedge around him, around his household, and around all that he has on every side? You have blessed the work of his hands, and his possessions have increased in the land"* (Job 1:10). Our physical eyes cannot see this hedge, but it is real without a doubt, and it exists in the spirit realm.

I believe that Job was protected not only because he was obedient, but he also regularly sacrificed animals to the Lord for the protection of his family: *"So it was, when the days of feasting had run their course, that Job would send and sanctify them, and he would rise early in the morning and offer burnt offerings according to the number of them all. For Job said, 'It may be that my sons have sinned and cursed God in their hearts.' Thus Job did regularly"* (Job 1:5). Job was protected through sacrificial blood.

The Bible clearly declares in Isaiah 54:17, *"No weapon formed against you shall prosper. And every tongue which rises against you in judgment you shall condemn; this is the heritage of the servants of the Lord and their righteousness is from me."*

We cannot prevent weapons being formed against us. But, if we are under the fortress-like safety of the blood of Jesus, any device of the enemy like magic, sorcery, witchcraft, and other weapons of destruction will prove powerless!

The devil can never approach us when the blood of Jesus is within and around us. The Bible says, *"For there is no sorcery against Jacob, nor any divination against Israel . . ."* (Numbers 23:23).

I would like to remind you of two more instances in the Bible where there was protection under the blood. Just before the Israelites left Egypt, the land faced the last plague of the death of all firstborn males. However, the Israelites were told to mark the doorposts of their home with the blood of a spotless lamb. Those who lived in homes that had the mark of blood on the doorposts were protected from death. The destroyer spared them (Exodus 12:13).

Similarly, when Jericho was being destroyed by the Israelites, Rahab and her household were the only ones under protection due to the red cord that was tied to the window of her house (Joshua 2:21, 6:25). In this instance, the color red signifies blood.

In the first instance of the Israelites, all the firstborn males in Egypt were killed—not by men—but by the destroyer. Here, the destruction was caused in the spiritual realm. In the case of Rahab, the people of Jericho were being killed by the Israelites—by men. This destruction was caused in the physical realm. These two incidents show us, without a shadow of doubt, that those who are covered by the blood are protected—both in the spiritual and physical realms!

If the blood of a goat or sheep, or just a red cord symbolizing blood can protect people from destruction, imagine the supernatural protection we have through the blood of Jesus Christ!

In a vision, the prophet Ezekiel heard the Lord instruct an angel to smite all the people who had turned to idolatry and to spare those who had the Lord's mark (Ezekiel 9:4-6). From this we know that in the spiritual realm, there is a shield of protection around God's children.

Psalm 91 talks about dwelling in the secret place and abiding under the shadow of the Almighty—a place where no enemy can approach us because we are safe under the blood of Jesus Christ. If we abide under His blood, we will have all the protection stated in this psalm. *"Surely He shall deliver you from the snare of the fowler, and from the perilous pestilence. He shall cover you with His feathers and under His wings you shall take refuge; His truth shall be your shield and buckler. You shall not be afraid of the terror by night; nor of the arrow that flies by day; Nor of the pestilence that walks in darkness; nor the destruction that lays waste at noonday. A thousand may fall at your side, and ten thousand at your right hand; but it shall not come near you. Only with your eyes shall you look, and see the reward of the wicked. Because you have made the LORD, who is my refuge, even the Most High, your dwelling place, No evil shall befall you, nor shall any plague come near your dwelling"* (Psalm 91:3-10).

While these references deal with the physical protection, the blood of Jesus also provides protection or pres-

The greatest protection the blood of Jesus gives us is protection for our souls.

ervation of our souls. The Bible tells us that the soul is more precious than all the riches in this world (Matthew 16:26; Mark 8:36), and that it lives forever (Matthew 10:28). Psalm 121:7 says, *"The Lord shall preserve you from all evil; He shall preserve your soul."* There are many other Scriptural promises assuring us that He will not leave the souls of His children in hell (Psalm 16:10, 56:13).

The greatest protection the blood of Jesus gives us is protection for our souls.

We can trust God's promise as in Zechariah 2:5: *"For I, says the Lord, will be a wall of fire all around her, and I will be the glory in her midst."*

Application:

Like the Israelites who smeared the blood of animals on their doors and doorposts, when you apply the blood of Jesus in faith—either by your word or by the sprinkling of water or oil—upon yourself, your family, your substance, and all things concerning you, you are sure to receive and enjoy God's total protection.

Let us, therefore, take refuge in the fortress-like protection of His blood. Jesus, the living rock, is our only refuge. Our lives, families, homes, business, ministries, and every possession will be under the protection of His blood. Neither Satan nor his followers can approach us. Only His blood can offer us absolute protection.

Prayer:

Heavenly Father, You alone have the power to protect Your people. I confess that You are my rock and strong fortress. By faith, I apply Jesus' blood on myself, my family, and on all that concerns us. Keep us from the wicked plans of the enemy that go against the amazing plans You have for us! I thank You, Lord, for Your supernatural protection. In the mighty name of our Lord and Savior, Jesus Christ, I pray. Amen!

Reflection:

What are the areas for which you need protection in your life?

Where does absolute protection come from and how can you obtain it?

The Blood of Jesus Heals

*"But He was wounded for our transgressions. He was bruised for our iniquities. The chastisement for our peace was upon Him, and **by His stripes we are healed**."*

– Isaiah 53:5 (emphasis added)

Key Point:

The blood of Jesus has not only washed away our sins, but has also made a way for our healing. The blood He shed for us has healed all ailments of the body and the mind. We are healed by His blood!

Message:

When Moses married an Ethiopian woman, Miriam and Aaron spoke against Moses. God called them to the tabernacle and said to Miriam and Aaron, *"Hear now My words: if there is a prophet among you, I, the LORD, make Myself known to him in a vision; I speak to him in a dream. Not so with My servant Moses; he is faithful in all My house. I speak with him face to face, even plainly, and not in dark sayings; and he sees the form of the LORD. Why then were you not afraid to speak against My servant Moses?"* (Numbers 12:6-8). Immediately, Miriam became leprous like snow. This clearly shows us that when we do what displeases God, or when we disobey God's Word, diseases come upon us.

In Numbers 25, we read about the men of Israel who indulged in sexual immorality with Moabite women and took part in the sacrificial meals, and also bowed down before their gods. This act of the Israelites kindled God's anger, and no fewer than 24,000 people were killed in the plague as a result of their sinful acts. This is an example of sin bringing a disease upon those who sinned. The plague ended only when Phinehas drove a spear into the offending couple in their tent. If the blood of those sinners had the power to halt an epidemic, it is beyond doubt that the blood of Jesus will heal us of our diseases and deliver us from the outcome of our transgressions.

As descendants of Adam and Eve, the seed of sin is born into us. When we see or hear wicked things, sinful thoughts are formed in our minds. When these thoughts begin to operate inside us, these thoughts lead us to the act of sin. For example, lustful thoughts often lead to adultery, which may result in sexually transmitted diseases, like AIDS. Sin causes disease, be it physical, emotional, or mental.

If the blood of Jesus Christ can forgive, cleanse and remove our sins, will not the same blood heal all diseases, which are an outcome of our sin? *"Who forgives all your iniquities, who heals all your diseases"* (Psalm 103:3). The Bible says that Jesus healed them all (Matthew 12:15).

In Isaiah 53:4 we read, *"Surely he hath born our griefs and carried our sorrows"* The Hebrew Word for grief is "choli" which also means sickness, affliction, disease, infirmities, illness and grief.[7]

When our Lord Jesus healed the sick, we read in the gospel of Matthew where the author refers to that very verse from Isaiah 53:4, *"That it might be fulfilled which was spoken by Isaiah the prophet, saying He Himself took our infirmities and bore our sickness"* (Matthew 8:17). Jesus fulfilled that prophetic word from Isaiah by bearing all our sickness and infirmities.

When the Roman soldiers scourged Jesus, pressed down a crown of thorns on His head, hit Him on His head with a rod, nailed His hands and feet to the cross and pierced His side with a spear, He bled from His wounds. Normally, after the blood stops flowing and the wounds start to heal, stripes or scars begin to form. In Isaiah 53:5, the prophet says, *"by His stripes we are healed,"* while Peter writing in 1 Peter 2:24 asserts that *"by whose stripes you were healed."* The scars on the body of Jesus are a testament to the fact that He carried all our diseases and sickness in order to bring healing to us. Just like a blood test is proof of the diseases a body may have, similarly the blood of Jesus is the proof that He carried all our diseases. He paid the penalty not only for our sin but also the consequence of sin, namely sickness and diseases. When we acknowledge the finished work on the cross and profess that the blood He shed was for our healing, we *will* experience the victorious healing power of His blood. *He is an unchanging God. He will surely heal you by the precious blood of Jesus Christ, even today.*

A few years ago, I developed a skin allergy. Swollen patches were visible all over my body. I consulted doctors, who advised me to avoid eating mutton (goat), and fish.

> *He is an unchanging God. He will surely heal you by the precious blood of Jesus Christ, even today.*

I avoided these foods for months, but to no avail. One day, I knelt down and prayed for complete healing. The Holy Spirit then reminded me to look to the blood of Jesus. He prompted me, and I started praying, "Wash me with your blood, cleanse me, heal me." In faith, I smeared His blood over my body. The healing started then, and gradually I received my complete healing. No more allergies! No more pain! Even now, I don't need to follow any diet restrictions.

My temporary struggles with what I could or couldn't eat reminded me of a meal of eternal significance. In 1 Corinthians 11:23-31, Paul talks about the Lord's Supper. This meal instituted by Jesus has the power to heal us, but we must posture ourselves to partake in it. In Paul's letter, we read about the suffering that comes upon one who takes part in the Lord's Supper in an unworthy manner. 1 Corinthians 11:30 says, *"For this reason, many are weak and sick among you, and many sleep."* But if we remember the suffering and death of Jesus and the penalty He paid for our sins, believing that His body and blood have the power to bring us blessing and healing, we can partake in the Lord's Supper with reverence and worthiness. And, we can receive healing through the blood of Jesus.

I once met a Christian woman who had been diagnosed with blood cancer. The cancer treatment caused her to lose all her hair. The doctors had confirmed that her days were numbered. Under these circumstances, she came to realize that only the blood of Jesus could heal and transform her

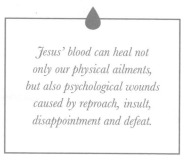

Jesus' blood can heal not only our physical ailments, but also psychological wounds caused by reproach, insult, disappointment and defeat.

blood. With this realization, she started partaking in the Lord's Supper. Amazingly, she received divine strength and healing. She is still alive today, serving the Lord and writing songs for Him.

This is not a one-off incident. Several people who were diagnosed with "incurable" diseases have received healing when they began receiving the Lord's communion with great faith. Most of them are still living for the glory of God! I am reminded of my own physical healing that came through praying the blood of Jesus over my life each time I partake of the Lord's supper. *Jesus' blood can heal not only our physical ailments, but also psychological wounds caused by reproach, insult, disappointment and defeat.*

Application:

You too might be suffering because of how others treat you. Perhaps a family member, colleague or superior in your office has let you down. Remember, Jesus has borne your griefs and carried your sorrows and said *"It is finished"* on the cross. Whatever your emotional wounds are, the blood of Jesus has the power to heal you right now. Believe God's Word and the work accomplished through His blood, and you will be healed right now. Jeremiah 33:6 gives us this assurance, *"Behold, I will bring it health and healing; I will heal them . . ."*

Prayer:

Dear Heavenly Father, I thank you for sending Your Son Jesus to shed His precious blood and heal all my diseases. I may have sickness and pain in my body and mind. Let each drop of blood that Jesus shed for me, flow through me and strengthen my body. Remove all my pain and heal me completely. I confess that I am now healed by the blood of Jesus. I thank You, Lord, for healing me. In the healing and restoring name of our Lord Jesus Christ, I pray. Amen!

Reflection:

Did God create man to suffer with sickness and diseases?

What did Jesus accomplish on the cross in order to heal your sickness and how can you appropriate God's healing in your life?

The Blood of Jesus Reveals His Word

*"He was **clothed with a robe dipped in blood**, and His name is called **The Word of God**."*

– Revelation 19:13 (emphasis added)

Key Point:

As we read the Word of God through the application of His blood, we will receive life-changing revelations.

Message:

A politician, who said he did not believe in God, won an election after several defeats. In his victory speech he said, *"For a righteous man may fall seven times and rise again."* Since he was quoting Proverbs 24:16, I presume that he had read the Bible.

People use the Bible for all kinds of reasons. Some read the Bible just to be able to quote the Word for their benefit. Some are curious and read the Bible just to find out what it says. Others read it just to find fault. Many Christians read the Bible out of habit. It becomes routine. However, seldom do people understand the revelations in God's Word. Whether educated or illiterate, no one can really understand the fullness of meaning God's word holds unless God reveals it. (Isaiah 29:11-12). And these revelations come through Jesus' blood.

A revelation about God is found in the first chapter of John's gospel: *"In the beginning was the Word, and the Word was with God, and the Word was God"* (John 1:1). *"And the Word became flesh and dwelt among us, and we beheld His glory, the glory as of the only begotten of the Father, full of grace and truth"* (John 1:14). Jesus Christ, the Son of God, is the Word of God made flesh. All revelations are hidden in God's Word. Therefore, we must know and understand Jesus, who is God's Word, in order to receive His blessings in our lives.

And not only is Jesus the Word of God, but his blood makes the promises of God come alive. Because Jesus shed His blood to establish the New Covenant, his blood ratifies this covenant and brings these promises to life. Matthew 26:28 says, *"For this is My blood of the new covenant, which [ratifies the agreement and] is being poured out for many for the forgiveness of sins"* (AMP).

The written word of God (logos) must become the spoken word of God (rhema). Rhema words provide counsel in our current situations, and help with decisions we make in our day-to-day lives. In bringing together these revelations from John and Matthew, we see how the

Word of God, both written in scriptures and made flesh in Christ, springs to life in us—only through the blood of Jesus.

On the island of Patmos, God gave the apostle John a wonderful vision, which he recorded in the book of Revelation. John says that in his vision, he saw someone sitting on a white horse—**with a name that no one knew except Himself.** Later on, John was able to identify the person's name as the *"Word of God."* Subsequently, he says that person's name is *KING OF KINGS AND LORD OF LORDS.*

He was able to read and recognize the name because the person on the white horse was wearing a robe dipped in blood. The blood of Jesus revealed the identity of God and the "Word of God" to John (Revelation 19:11-16). *I believe that even today,*

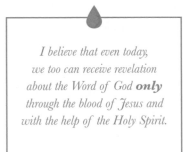

*I believe that even today, we too can receive revelation about the Word of God **only** through the blood of Jesus and with the help of the Holy Spirit.*

*we too can receive revelation about the Word of God **only** through the blood of Jesus and with the help of the Holy Spirit.*

Many years ago, God gave me a wonderful revelation on Psalm 35:27. *"Let them shout for joy and be glad, who favor my righteous cause; And let them say continually, 'Let the Lord be magnified, Who has pleasure in the prosperity of His servant.'"* From this I understood that God delights in the wellbeing or prosperity of His servants. This revelational word transformed my life and ministry. Today, God has made me a blessing to many people. Like me, there are many others who have received a revelation from the Word of God, and have gone on to do great exploits for our Lord.

Because of the blood of Jesus, we see God's word revealed. Like John identified the figure on the white horse as the Word of God because of the blood on His robe, we can receive the revelations of God's written Word because of Jesus' blood.

Application:

The Bible is the written Word, which brings transformation and blessing because it holds life. The secret to

One revelation from God can change your destiny.

finding this everlasting life in the Word is the blood of Jesus. Therefore, as you read the Word, let it cleanse your eyes and mind by His blood, so that you will be able to receive insight and revelation into His Word. *One revelation from God can change your destiny.*

It is time for us to return to foundational truths. Let us realign our lives by appropriating the sacrifice of Jesus on the cross. Then we will discover that every word of God is real and full of life. Revelatory knowledge will flow like a river.

May our Lord give you more revelations in His Word!

Prayer:

Dear Lord God, thank You for helping me to understand that You are the Word, and that all life is found in You and in Your Word. Wash my mind, eyes and ears with Your precious blood so that I can receive fresh insights into Your Word. Let Your revelatory knowledge manifest in my life so I may build my life and the lives of others around me. Thank You for Your blood and the cross. In the revelatory name of Jesus Christ, I pray. Amen!

Reflection:

Have you really asked God to reveal the Scriptures to you?

What is the impact of God's revelation through His Word in your life?

The Blood of Jesus Inspires to Create

*"And **they sang a new song**, saying: "You are worthy to take the scroll, And to open its seals; For You were slain, **And have redeemed us to God by Your blood** out of every tribe and tongue and people and nation."*

— Revelation 5:9 (emphasis added)

Key Point:

God was and is the greatest Creator. Now, the blood of Jesus, which inspires creativity, flows through us. Because of it, we can sing new songs and create new things, through which others can see the glory of God, the Creator.

Message:

While he was on the island of Patmos, the apostle John received a vision from God, which has been recorded in the book of Revelation. In his vision, John saw a Person seated on the throne, holding a scroll in His right hand. The Lamb then took the scroll from the Person who was seated on the throne. Four living creatures and the twenty-four elders fell down before the Lamb, and they sang a new song.

John heard every creature in heaven and on earth and under the earth and in the sea singing, *"To Him who sits on the throne and to the Lamb be praise and honor and glory and power forever and ever!"* On hearing this song, the four living creatures said *"Amen"* and the elders fell down and worshipped (Revelation 5:8-14, NIV).

From this vision, we see that the angels, the elders, the redeemed people and all of God's creation sang new songs as an act of adoration to the Lamb of God (Revelation 5:9). Yes, the blood of Christ redeemed them, and they sang new songs to Him. We can say that the blood inspired them to sing a new song.

Many years ago, a friend invited me to an art exhibition that he had organized. He introduced me to the artist whose work was on display. I had an opportunity to talk to him. He seemed gentle and well mannered. My friend asked the artist if he would like me to pray for him. He replied, "Of course. I would be glad to receive a blessing." The moment I closed my eyes and started to pray for him, I heard a loud scream. I opened my eyes and I saw this gentle, well-mannered man yelling while tearing at his coat and tie.

Immediately, I rebuked the spirit that was tormenting him and commanded it to leave him in the name of Jesus.

The evil spirit replied, "Why are you chasing me out? It was he (the artist) who invited me in. I give him inspiration to create art." After the prayer, the artist was delivered from the evil spirit. His countenance was totally changed and there was a glow on his face. Praise the Lord!

When I think about this incident, I realize how very surprised I am by the statement made by the evil spirit. The Bible tells us that our God, Elohim, is the One who created the universe and the earth. He created every visible and invisible thing, beautifully.

But even when Moses performed signs and wonders before Pharaoh to prove the one True God of the Israelites, the magicians of Egypt also managed to perform the same miracles! They were able to deceive Pharaoh and the people (Exodus 7:22). The devil is a deceiver and a counterfeit. He too performs wonders, but they always *imitate* the miracles of God. God Almighty is the one and only true Creator (Genesis 1:1; Nehemiah 9:6; Psalm 148:4-5; Isaiah 66:2; Ecclesiastes 3:11; Revelation 4:11). Satan always tries to claim and copy what belongs to God (Isaiah 14:13-14). Satan (Lucifer) is a created being, so he can *never* possess the attributes of the Creator God.

Furthermore, in Exodus 7:11-12, we see that Moses, through God's power, turned water into blood and brought frogs out of the rivers. The magicians performed both these miracles too, but through a power that was NOT from God. They could do them because these miracles were an outcome of something that already existed, i.e. water turning into blood and frogs coming out of the rivers. However, after these two, they could not replicate

> *Just the finger of God is enough to bring down the kingdom of the devil!*

any more miracles, because the further plagues on the Egyptians were an original creation of God—created out of nothing! It was supernatural. Even the magicians acknowledged that "this is the finger of God." *Just the finger of God is enough to bring down the kingdom of the devil!*

The devil can only duplicate and replicate things. He can never create new things, because that authority and power lies only with our YHWH.

Some people, like the artist I prayed for, seek Satan for inspiration—to write songs, make movies or design new products. Their only motive is to become rich and famous. In the process they, either knowingly or unknowingly, sell their souls to the devil. Often, the end of their life is pathetic. They may have been famous, but they eventually become lonely and depressed. They often live in constant fear. Some even become insane. Very often, it ends up with them committing suicide.

But we know that these evil spirits imitating God do not have the final word. Jesus came into this world to reveal God. While He walked this earth, He performed many creative miracles. Here are some examples:

- Jesus took five loaves and two fish and multiplied them to feed five thousand men, not including women and children (Matthew 14:15-21).

- Jesus used a silver coin taken from the mouth of a fish to pay His taxes (Matthew 17:24-27).
- Jesus touched a leper and he was made whole (Matthew 8:2-4).
- Jesus healed a blind man at Bethsaida (Mark 8:22-26).
- Jesus restored a crippled hand (Mark 3:1-5).
- Jesus raised Lazarus from the dead four days after he was placed in the tomb (John 11:1-46).

Jesus, who created all things, is the same yesterday, today and forever (Hebrews 13:8). God is still creating now. For example, every newborn baby is a creation of God (Psalm 127:3, 139:14). Every new believer is a creation of God. He creates a new heart in everyone who responds to His call (Ezekiel 36:26). He is creating the New Jerusalem (Revelation 21:1-5).

Can you stop someone who has a passion to create? No! Our God loves creating new things. Would He quit now? No way! God always wants to create.

Application:

It is in God's nature to create. His passion to create is found in the blood of Jesus. That blood runs through your veins. When you start fully comprehending the sacrifice of Jesus, the Lamb of God, inspiration to create erupts from your heart—sometimes in the form of music. You may not be a great musician or songwriter, but the blood of Jesus in you brings out a new song. This is why we have so many new worship songs in recent years. The blood of Jesus is taking the church to higher levels of worship.

Do you have the desire to write new songs, create music, or create other things for His glory? Seek Elohim, the true Creator, and not Satan, the counterfeiter. Repent for your ignorance and seek His forgiveness. Ask God to wash you by His blood. When you truly start admiring His sacrifice for you on the cross, your heart and mind will be filled with inspiration to write new songs. Seek Him, and He will surely fulfill your heart's desire. The blood of Elohim, the Creator, is in you; He will create things for you and through you.

Prayer:

Dear Heavenly Father, You are the Creator. You have created everything so beautifully. You have a passion to create and are always creating something new. Through Your Son Jesus, You have revealed this to us. Having understood this truth, I now seek You with all my heart. Immerse my heart and mind in the precious blood of Jesus. Let Your blood bestow the ability to create. Let Your blood help me sing new songs so that I may worship You in the beauty of Your holiness. Lord, create in me a new heart. Help me to create new things that bring glory to Your name. In the inspirational name of our Lord Jesus, I pray. Amen!

Reflection:

What do you understand about God's name: *Elohim*?

How can this name make a difference in your life?

The Blood of Jesus Empowers

*"To Him who loved us and washed us from our sins **in His own blood, and has made us kings and priests** to His God and Father, to Him be glory and dominion forever and ever. Amen."*

– Revelation 1:5-6 (emphasis added)

Key Point:

The blood of Jesus has made us Kings and Priests in His Kingdom. We can use our authority and seize our blessings!

Message:

Once I had booked tickets on a flight from Malaysia to Singapore, and then onwards to Chennai, India. The flight from Malaysia was scheduled to depart at 6:50 p.m., and the flight from Singapore to Chennai was scheduled to depart at 8:35 p.m. I needed to be in Chennai to address a gathering the next day. However, the flight from Malaysia was postponed to 7:30 p.m., and although we reached Singapore by 8:15 p.m., our plane remained in the air, circling the airport, since there was no landing slot available.

At that moment, I realized in faith that I had power as a redeemed person washed by the blood of Jesus. I declared to myself, "Scripturally, I am a king and whatever I say will happen!" I continued to declare: "Today the plane scheduled to leave at 8:35 p.m. will not leave this airport before I board it!"

The plane I was on landed in Singapore only at 8:30 p.m. By the time I got off the plane, it was already 8:45 p.m. I rushed towards the plane for Chennai. Wonder of wonders—it was still there! As soon as I boarded the plane, the doors shut behind me. That flight took off at 9:00 p.m., and I arrived in time to preach the Word of God in Chennai the next day. Hallelujah!

Ecclesiastes 8:4 says, *"Where the word of a king is, there is power . . ." By His blood Jesus Christ has made us kings and priests, vesting in us the authority of a king and priest!*

According to the Old Testament, once a year, after all the rituals were completed, the high priest would sprinkle the blood of the sacrifice on the Ark of the Covenant for the atonement of the sins of the people. This sprinkled blood would remain upon the Ark of the Covenant. Apart from the golden jar holding the manna, Aaron's rod which budded, and

> *By His blood Jesus Christ has made us kings and priests, vesting in us the authority of a king and priest!*

the tablets of the covenant (Hebrews 9:4), that sacrificial blood was also on that Ark of the Covenant. And when the priests carried the Ark around, miracles happened for God's children! We see that the river Jordan gave way for them to pass through, the walls of Jericho came crashing down, and even wars were won by the Israelites—just to name a few of the miracles! *The power of the blood has been concealed in the Old Testament but revealed in the New Testament.*

When we are redeemed by the blood of Jesus, we become the bone of His bones and the flesh of His flesh. We become one in Spirit with Him, and our life is hidden in Him (Ephesians 5:30; 1 Corinthians 6:17; Colossians 3:3). Our filthy garments have been removed, and the garment of glory is upon us, as priests in His kingdom (Exodus 28:2; Zechariah 3:4-5). Our Lord has raised us and made us to sit in the heavenly places

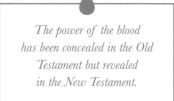

The power of the blood has been concealed in the Old Testament but revealed in the New Testament.

(Ephesians 2:6). We are not only seated with Jesus in heavenly places, but we have also been made kings and priests in the kingdom of God (Revelation 1:5-6). We are no longer slaves or insignificant people, but are chosen ones who are bestowed with power and authority.

After Jesus' resurrection, His blood was transported to the true sanctuary in heaven where it exists as eternal atonement for the sins of the world. When His blood washes us, we are also transported and seated above. Furthermore, after Jesus' death and resurrection and before

His ascension, Jesus told His disciples, *"All authority has been given to Me in heaven and earth"* (Matthew 28:18). The devil may have authority over this earth (Luke 4:5-6), but our Lord has all authority over heaven and earth. It is evident that God's authority is far greater than that of the devil.

Application:

We see in the Old Testament that the prayer of the high priest was special to God. His words brought results and blessings in peoples' lives (1 Samuel 1:17; Numbers 6:22-27). By the blood of Jesus, we too have been bestowed with the authority of kings and priests. When we plead the blood, we are connected to the highest source of power—God in heaven. That is why when we command, demons will flee, the wall of obstacles will be broken, a way will be made where there is no way, and we will have absolute victory over our enemies.

When we accept Jesus as our personal Savior, He gives us the mighty authority that He earned for us through His blood.

- *"Behold, I give you the authority to trample on serpents and scorpions, and over all the power of the enemy, and nothing shall by any means hurt you"* (Luke 10:19).
- *"You shall tread upon the lion and the cobra, the young lion and the serpent you shall trample underfoot"* (Psalm 91:13).
- *"Assuredly, I say to you, whatever you bind on earth will be bound in heaven, and whatever you loose on earth will be loosed in heaven"* (Matthew 18:18).

When you pray to bind the works of the devil, they will be bound in the spiritual realm first. As a result of the spiritual binding, they are bound in the physical realm also. In the same way, when you pray releasing anything, it will be released in the spiritual realm first, and as a result of the spiritual release, it will also be released in the physical realm.

Yes, beloved! Whatever we bind in prayer on this earth will be bound in heaven. Whatever we loose here will be loosed in heaven also. If the blessings that you ought to receive are held up by the devil, you can release them by prayer, claiming the power of the blood of Jesus.

We have the God-given authority to bind the actions of the devil, the ruler of this world. Let us exercise this mighty power. Because of the ignorance of this marvelous truth, many believers suffer a lot, both spiritually and physically.

Let us receive and enjoy the blessings as we are made kings and priests by the blood of Jesus. Let us make those around us prosper through this power granted by God!

Prayer:

Dear Almighty God, You empower Your people. Thank you, Jesus, for washing me with Your blood and making me a king and a priest. Thank You for giving me power through Your blood. In Your name, I bind all the evil forces that work against me, my family, my business and my ministry. In Your precious name, I release peace, joy, good health, finances, a godly partner, godly seed and a godly family, a better way of life and all other blessings which You want to bestow on me. Let all these blessings flow into my life unhindered by the evil one. Thank you, Lord, for answering my prayers. In the name of Jesus Christ, the King of kings and the Lord of lords, I pray. Amen!

Reflection:

What is your spiritual position now? Are you burdened or empowered?

How do you exercise your authority to seize your blessings?

The Blood of Jesus Destroys the Enemy's Strategy

"[God] disarmed the principalities and powers that were ranged against us and made a bold display and public example of them, in triumphing over them in Him and in it [the cross]."

– Colossians 2:15 (AMPC)

Key Point:

The blood of Jesus has nullified every plan of Satan against us. By His blood, we will be preserved, and we will see the destruction of our enemies.

Message:

The Bible tells us that the Old Testament is a *shadow* of the things to come (Colossians 2:17). Much of what was prophesied about in the Old Testament is fulfilled in the New Testament when our Lord was born in this world. Satan had a strategy to destroy Jesus while He was in the world; he induced King Herod to kill all the male children, from two years old to newborn, in and around Bethlehem (Matthew 2:16); he provoked the people's mind to cast Jesus down from the brow of the steep hill (Luke 4:29-30); he filled the minds of the people to stone Jesus to death (John 8:59;10:31-39). But the devil could not do anything to Jesus.

However, at the appointed time of God, Jesus allowed the soldiers to apprehend Him. Jesus was beaten and tortured by the Roman soldiers and other authorities. We know that these torturous acts were done under the influence of Satan (See John 13:2, 27; 2 Corinthians 4:4). There was motive behind every wound that was inflicted on

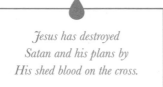

Jesus has destroyed Satan and his plans by His shed blood on the cross.

our Lord. For example, when the Roman soldier pierced Jesus' side to know whether he was dead on the cross or not (John 19:34), I believe that was Satan's attempt to subvert the story of Eve's creation. Satan knew that God took the rib from the side of Adam and created Eve. It is possible that Satan would have thought that Jesus' bride may come from His side, as Eve did from the first Adam. And indeed, when Jesus shed the last drop of blood from His side, His bride, the Church, was birthed. And the Bible confirms that God purchased the church by Jesus' blood (Acts 20:28). *Jesus has destroyed Satan and his plans by His shed blood on the cross.*

At the same time, the Bible warns about Satan's devices (2 Corinthians 2:11) and states that our adversary, the devil, prowls around like a roaring lion, seeking someone to devour (1 Peter 5:8).

Ephesians 6:12 reminds us that we are fighting against a well-organized, spiritual enemy: *"For we are not fighting against flesh-and-blood enemies, but against evil rulers and authorities of the unseen world, against mighty powers in this dark world, and against evil spirits in the heavenly places"* (NLT). It is not only Satan and his subordinates who attack us, but also people in this world who are under his influence.

In the book of Job, we read that Satan had to obtain permission from God to attack Job. Satan had a strategy. He used people as well as nature to systematically steal, kill, and destroy Job's family and wealth (Job 1:13-19). And to top things off, Satan struck Job with terrible sores. Job was covered in ulcers and scabs from head to foot (Job 2:7).

In Luke 22:31-32, we read that Satan had planned to sift Jesus' disciple Peter as wheat. Satan seeks to distract and distress those who are following and pursuing God wholeheartedly. He takes what gives us life and seeks to steal, kill, and destroy it.

Beloved people of God, there is an ongoing battle in life every day. Do not forget that the strategies of Satan are cunning and his intentions are cruel. Several casualties already have their bones strewn in the valley. Many others have been wounded. Only very few have experienced victory. Remember that Satan, the ruler of this world, is the one who schemes these conflicts of life using his dangerous weapons. But by the grace of God, we will overcome him. It is only the knowledge of Christ's crucifixion and the benefits that we derive from it that give us victory. Therefore, let us now see how we can overpower the Enemy's strategies!

Satan, with all his knowledge and experience, carefully planned and crucified Jesus. The Word of God speaks of God's hidden wisdom, *"which none of the rulers of this age knew; for had they known, they would not have crucified the Lord of glory"* (1 Corinthians 2:8). Certainly, Satan made a poor decision. The blood of Jesus confused him and his plans. Satan did not expect Jesus to bring salvation to mankind through His blood, but that's exactly what Jesus did. It is impossible for any of God's created beings to comprehend His divine wisdom.

Our Lord Jesus defeated and destroyed Satan physically on the cross and stripped all the spiritual tyrants in the universe of their sham authority and schemes (Colossians 2:14-15; Hebrews 2:14; 1 John 3:8). The blood of Jesus is the evidence of Satan's total destruction.

In 2 Kings 3, we read that when the Moabites saw the water as red as blood, they thought the kings of their enemies had killed each other and that the land was covered with blood (verse 23). Then they made the fateful decision to leave their fortified city. Instead of defending themselves, they attacked the Israelites, which led to their destruction. We could say they dug their own graves.

The spiritual significance here is that when we are under the blood of Jesus, His blood wages our battles for us. Though our Enemy and the evil powers of the world have different strategies to attack and destroy us, they will always fail when we are under Jesus' blood.

Very early one morning in 2006, just as I was about to get out of bed, I saw Satan coming at me with a big knife. I quickly moved aside and the blade of the knife missed me. I escaped by a hair's breadth! I opened my eyes with a sense of relief and took a deep breath. But as I shut my eyes again for a moment, I realized it wasn't over. This time, I saw Satan trying to attack me with seven sharp knives! I couldn't run from it. It was a really frightening experience. I opened my eyes and wondered what these attacks meant.

A few months later, there was a seven-fold attack on my family and me. These attacks had a devastating impact on our lives. Later, I understood that Satan had planned the seven specific attacks on us, and the visions were an indication of those attacks. When I started to apply the blood of Jesus on our lives, my outlook changed. Though we went through a very rough time, we were able to overcome our adversaries by the grace of God.

Application:

In this world, the Enemy and his followers may have strategies to destroy you, but God has a master plan to counter them all, and He will bring them to defeat! *When we plead the blood of Jesus, God will turn adverse situations around for our own good and His glory.*

Prayer:

Dear Heavenly Father, I thank You for the blood of Your Son, Jesus. Accept me as I am with my flaws. Cleanse my unclean heart, and wash me with Your blood. Let your blood cover my entire family and me. Nullify the strategies and attacks of my enemies against me and all that concerns me. Whatever the Enemy has planned, I know You can turn it around for my good and for Your glory. Thank You, Lord, for hearing my prayer and for the manifested presence of Your blood in my life. I pray this in the all-powerful name of our Lord Jesus Christ, Amen!

Reflection:

What was Satan's plan and how did Jesus thwart it?

How can you nullify Satan's strategies in your life?

Part five

The Inheritance

The Blood of Jesus Brings the Presence of God

"Repent therefore and be converted, that your sins may be blotted out, so that times of refreshing may come from the presence of the Lord."

— Acts 3:19

Key Point:

The blood of Jesus has given us access to enter into the presence of the Holy God. His blood brings down His presence among us, and God's presence stays with us wherever we go. It helps us hear Him clearly. What an amazing blessing that is!

Message:

In 19th century India, there lived a mighty man of God. He walked from Kashmir, in the northern most part of India, to Kanyakumari in the southern tip, and proclaimed the gospel of Jesus Christ.

His ministry was accepted only in some places; in other places, he was beaten and sometimes imprisoned. Recently, when people were cleaning one of the cells where he had been imprisoned, they found a copy of the New Testament. In it was a note that read, "The presence of God changed this dark cell into a glorious place for me."

Yes, my beloved, wherever the presence of God is, that place becomes glorious. The blood of Jesus brings the presence of God into our lives. Before we meditate on this, let us see how blood brought God's presence into the midst of the Israelites.

In Exodus 24:3-8, we read how Moses built an altar and sacrificed oxen as offerings to the Lord. Moses took half of the blood and sprinkled it on the altar. The other half he sprinkled on all the people (Hebrews 9:19). We can visualize this scene at the foot of Mount Sinai—half of the blood sprinkled over three million people, and the other half poured on the altar. If *half* the blood of an ox was poured on the altar, streams of blood would have surely flowed down! The altar must have been engulfed in blood. In these circumstances, Moses, Aaron, Aaron's sons Nadab and Abihu, and the seventy elders of the Israelites went up to Mount Sinai and met the God of Israel. All the Israelites saw the glory of God resting on Mount Sinai.

The Lord who dwells in the heavens said to Moses, *"And let them make Me a sanctuary, that I may dwell among them"* (Exodus 25:8). And as a result of the blood offering, God's presence came down and dwelt among the Israelites. *If the blood of mere animals poured on the altar could usher in the presence of the Lord, how much more can the blood of Jesus Christ do to bring God's presence into our midst!*

God's presence also dwelt among the Israelites in the tabernacle. When God delivered the Israelites from Egypt, Moses built the tabernacle according to the pattern shown to him on Mount Sinai (Exodus 25:40; Hebrews 8:5). As we already saw, there was a fence that surrounded the tabernacle. The place before you entered the tabernacle was called the outer court.

The tabernacle itself had two chambers, divided by two veils—one at the entrance of the tabernacle, and another just before the Holy of Holies (Exodus 36:35; 2 Chronicles 3:14). Only the priests were allowed to come into the Holy Place. And in Holy of Holies where the presence of God dwelt, only the high priest could enter in—

> *If the blood of mere animals poured on the altar could usher in the presence of the Lord, how much more can the blood of Jesus Christ do to bring God's presence into our midst!*

and only once a year. The priest would go in with the blood, which was offered for himself and for the sins of the people (Hebrews 9:7). It is in that most Holy Place that the Almighty God communes with man; *"And there I will meet with you, and I will speak with you from above the mercy seat, from between the two cherubim which are on the ark of the Testimony, about everything which I will give you in commandment to the children of Israel"* (Exodus 25:22).

There was a veil that kept the Holy Place separate from the people. But when the Son of God, Jesus, shed His blood on the cross, the veil of the temple was "rent in twain," meaning torn in two from top to bottom (Matthew 27:51). With His blood, Jesus Christ, the Most High Priest, removed the veil that was blocking the glorious presence of God.

When I spoke on the blessings of the blood of Jesus in my friend's church, the entire congregation experienced God's glorious presence. They later shared their testimonies. When I wait on the Lord, and meditate particularly on the blood of Jesus, I feel His awesome presence.

A man I know, after reading the manuscript of this very book, testified that he and his wife felt a light spray descending upon them when they prayed together for the precious blood of Jesus to come into their marriage and family life.

Application:

When you receive Jesus as your personal Savior, His blood washes you. You become a member of His body, His flesh and His bones (Ephesians 5:30). And you too can enter into the glorious presence of God (Hebrews 4:16). We are no longer kept out of God's presence by a veil. Yes! It is the blood of Jesus that makes the way for us to enter into God's presence.

Throughout the scriptures, we see how Christ's blood makes way for God's presence. When we are washed by

His blood, new songs will spontaneously burst out in our heart (Revelation 5:9). This adoration brings down the presence of God (Psalm 22:3). In His presence, there is fullness of joy (Psalm16:11). It is here that we can hear His voice (Exodus 25:22). Though David was king of the land and had all the pleasures of this world at his disposal, he yearned deeply for God's presence. He understood that true and complete joy could be found only in God's presence, and not in anything the world could offer. It was there that David could hear God's voice in, and through him. In the psalms that were written by David, we can see how God spoke to and through David—especially about the coming of the Messiah.

David pens in Psalm 27:4, *"One thing I have desired of the Lord, that will I seek: that I may dwell in the house of the Lord all the days of my life, to behold the beauty of the Lord, and to inquire in His temple."*

What a privilege it is for us to be able to enter into God's presence through the blood of Jesus! His presence remains with us wherever we go. His presence surrounds us. Above all, when we are in His presence, joy bubbles over in our spirit, and we will be able to hear His voice clearly. What greater blessing can there be?

Prayer:

Dear Father God, You delight to dwell among Your people! You were a pillar of cloud and fire while leading the Israelites out of Egypt. I yearn for that presence, Lord! I thank You for Your presence, which is available to Your children through the blood of Jesus. Wash me in the precious blood of Jesus Christ and let Your presence surround me. Lead me in my journey through life and let Your presence go with me always. Help me hear Your voice clearly. In the amazing and astonishing name of our Savior, Jesus Christ, I pray. Amen!

Reflection:

How can we enter the presence of God?

What will be the outcome of entering God's presence in our day-to-day life?

The Blood of Jesus Gives New Life

> *"Therefore, since we are **now justified,** (acquitted, made righteous and brought into right relationship with God) **by Christ's blood . . ."***

– Romans 5:9 (AMP, emphasis added)

Key Point:

The blood of Jesus has made us new. Old things have been erased and removed completely. No one can condemn us of sins that are already forgiven! We can now live a life of fullness and blessing as new creations in Christ!

Message:

I once visited a hospital to pray for an elderly man. His wife, who was in the room, did something wrong. Triggered by it, the elderly man scolded her, recounting all her wrongdoings ever since their wedding day. As soon as he finished, his wife did the same, and pointed out all of his wrongdoings. This continued for a while, each taking turns to berate the other.

This couple had been married for more than fifty years. They had a large family, with children and grandchildren, and yet both of them kept a detailed account of each other's wrongdoings, item by item. They had them engraved in their hearts! I was deeply pained to witness this.

Thankfully, this is not the case with our wrongdoings. When a person confesses his sins, and is washed by Jesus' blood, he becomes a renewed person. *Jesus not only forgives our sins but He also forgets them forever.*

- *"I, even I, am He who blots out your transgression for My own sake; And I will not remember your sins"* (Isaiah 43:25).
- *"For I will be merciful to their unrighteousness, and their sins and their lawless deeds I will remember no more"* (Hebrews 8:12).

Our God *blots out* all our transgressions and does not bring them up ever again. But many people cannot forget their own sins—even those they have already confessed, even sins that have already been forgiven. They are unhappy and feel guilty about the sins that God Himself has forgotten. They are unable to forgive themselves.

> *Jesus not only forgives our sins but He also forgets them forever.*

Working subtly, the devil takes advantage of people's attitude towards their already forgiven sins. He brings their sins to remembrance—again and again. He constantly accuses them. His accusations soar high: "You have been unfaithful to your loving husband or wife. You have sinned against your children. You have betrayed your boss. You have sinned against God. You are unworthy to serve the Lord as His servant. You cannot receive grace from God for your sin is so grave." The list can go on and on. The devil's only aim is to find some means of taking away your faith in God. But we should never listen to the devil since he is a liar and the father of lies (John 8:44).

We must recognize two basic strategies of the devil. First, he deceives a person. We see this in the lives of Adam and Eve; the devil deceived them into eating the forbidden fruit. Once a person yields to the devil's deception and sins, he resorts to the second strategy—accusation. Deception and accusation are the two weapons the devil uses against us again and again.

Satan deceived Judas Iscariot into betraying His Lord, Jesus Christ. After the crucifixion of Christ, Satan, who turned Judas into a betrayer, was the same person who accused him and made him feel guilty for what he had done. This ultimately drove Judas Iscariot to suicide. As we saw above, the devil uses deception and accusation against people! He not only accuses us through our own conscience, but he also accuses us in God's presence. But his accusations have no power against the children of God who have been washed by the blood. There is no condemnation to those who are in Christ (Romans 8:1, 33-34)!

Years ago, I read the story of a lady who had lived a very immoral life in her past. By the grace of God, her life was totally transformed by the power of God. She became a minister of God, and is now making a big impact in many people's lives around the world. Her life shows that God can totally nullify our past and give us brand new lease on life.

The Scripture says that our Lord Jesus Christ has cleansed us by His blood. When we are washed by His blood, we become new creations—without any blemish! 2 Corinthians 5:17 says, *"Therefore, if anyone is in Christ, he is a new creation; old things have passed away; behold, all things have become new."* Our Lord has also given us a brand-new heart and spirit. *"I will give you a new heart and put a new spirit within you; I will take the heart of stone out of your flesh and give you a heart of flesh"* (Ezekiel 36:26). If that is so, why should we waste our life brooding over our confessed and blotted-out sins and the things which happened in our past?

Application:

Do not be ignorant of the Word of God any longer! Now that you know the truth, that truth will set you free (John 8:32). Let us no more believe the lies of the devil, but place our faith squarely on the Word of God. We can be totally free from the devil's bondages of deception and accusation!

According to Romans 3:24-26, 5:9 (AMP), we are

made righteous by the blood of Jesus Christ. The blood of Jesus has cleansed us, who were wallowing in the miry clay of sin. We are now considered as righteous in Christ. *God does not see us as condemned sinners but as righteous saints.*

What a great privilege it is to be seen as righteous before a Holy God! The blessings that we can receive from Him when we have the right standing with Him are numerous. The

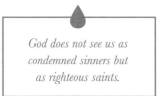

God does not see us as condemned sinners but as righteous saints.

blood of Jesus has renewed us. We have been made a new creation by His blood. The old has passed away, and all things are made new!

Prayer:

Dear God Almighty, thank You for removing all my wrongdoings, and making me righteous through Jesus' blood. I know that You have forgiven my sins, and that I cannot be condemned by anything that I did in the past. Let me not dwell on my past. Help me to lead a renewed life from this day. I surrender my future into Your hands, because I have been purchased by the blood of Jesus! I am a new creation and I belong to You! In the rejuvenating name of Jesus Christ our Lord, I pray. Amen!

Reflection:

Write the reasons for not being able to comprehend the new life bestowed on your life by Jesus.

How would you describe your identity in Christ and why is that identity important in your daily life?

The Blood of Jesus Will Bring Salvation to Your family

"Believe on the Lord Jesus Christ, and thou shalt be saved, and thy house."

– Acts 16:31 (KJV)

Key Point:

The blood of Jesus that has saved us will surely save all the members of our families!

Message:

While Moses was tending his flock in the desert, the Angel of the Lord appeared to him in the midst of a burning bush. He was given a great mission to deliver the Israelites from the hand of Pharaoh, and to bring them out of Egypt and into a land flowing with milk and honey.

As Moses was traveling to Egypt with his family, the Lord God appeared to him and tried to kill him (Exodus 4:24). But Zipporah, his wife, took a flint knife, cut off her son's foreskin and touched the feet of Moses with it saying, *"Surely you are a bridegroom of blood to me!"* So, the Lord God did not kill Moses (Exodus 4:25-26, NIV).

Why did God try to kill Moses? God made a covenant with Abraham and his descendants that every male among them would be circumcised. This was the sign of the covenant between God and Abraham (Genesis 17:10-11). God said that any uncircumcised male would be cut off from his people, because of the broken covenant (Genesis 17:14).

Many Bible scholars believe that even though Moses was a man called and divinely commissioned by God, He tried to kill Moses because he had not circumcised his son. Hence, we see that it is mandatory to obey all the commandments of the Lord in order to fulfill the call of ministry.

Let us look at this incident from a different perspective. When Zipporah cut the foreskin of her son, surely blood would have been shed—the blood of her son, who was born of her blood and the blood of Moses. That's why Zipporah said, *"Surely you are a bridegroom of blood to me!"* We can also say that Moses' life was spared, not only because of compliance to God's law, but the blood of his son that was shed also worked in his favor. The family was saved from destruction.

The CEV translation of Exodus 4:25-26 makes this

fact very clear. After Zipporah circumcised her son, she said, "'*My dear son, this blood will protect you.*' *So, the Lord did not harm Moses. Then Zipporah said, 'Yes, my dear, you are safe because of this circumcision.*'"

The word salvation comes from the Greek word "soteria" which also means protection, healing, prosperity. If the blood of Moses' son could bring salvation (and protection, in this case) to Moses and his family, how much more will the blood of our Savior Jesus Christ bring salvation to us!

We see several other key examples of the faith of one person saving entire families throughout Scripture. In the days of Noah, the wickedness of man had increased so much on the earth that God wanted to wipe out all mankind. But Noah found favor in the eyes of the Lord (Genesis 6:8). Because of Noah, his entire family was saved (Hebrews 11:7).

As Jesus passed through Jericho, Zacchaeus, a notoriously wealthy tax collector, being of short stature, ran ahead and climbed a sycamore tree to get a glimpse of Jesus. Jesus noticed him and went on to visit his home that day. The encounter with Jesus completely altered the infamous man. Seeing his transformation, Jesus did not say, "You are saved." Rather, Jesus said, "*Today salvation has come to this house, because he also is a son of Abraham;*" (Luke 19:9).

Cornelius, a Roman centurion, invited the apostle Simon Peter to his home, after God told him to do so in a vision. When he and those of his household heard Peter share the gospel truth of what Jesus had accomplished on the cross, the whole family was saved and baptized in water and in the Holy Spirit. Cornelius' obedience to the words of the angel of the Lord resulted in the salvation of his whole family.

Lydia, a believer and worshipper, was a dealer in purple cloth in Thyatira. While she was listening to the Apostle Paul's message, the Lord opened her heart, and ultimately, she *and her household* were baptized (Acts 16:14-15).

Paul and Silas were in prison in Philippi, praying and singing hymns to God. Around midnight, an earthquake shook the foundations of the prison. The prison doors flew open and everybody's chains were loosed. When the jailer woke up and saw the prison doors open, he drew his sword to kill himself because he thought all the

> *When one member receives salvation through the blood of Jesus Christ, the whole household receives the grace to be saved.*

prisoners had escaped. Paul shouted, *"Don't harm yourself. We are all here!"* The jailer called for lights, rushed in and fell trembling before Paul and Silas. He brought them out and asked, *"Sirs, what must I do to be saved?"* They replied, *"Believe in the Lord Jesus and you will be saved, you and your household"* (Acts 16:28, 30-31, NIV). *When one member receives salvation through the blood of Jesus Christ, the whole household receives the grace to be saved.*

Jesus was taken to Golgotha where He was beaten, whipped, crowned with thorns and forced to carry a huge cross on His shoulders. On the way to Golgotha, He met a man named Simon from Cyrene, who was also forced to carry the cross for a while. Surely, blood from Jesus' body would have been smeared on the cross, and some of that blood must have touched Simon's body.

After Jesus' ascension, the apostles began preaching the gospel as the Lord had commanded. The early apostles, who were true witnesses for the Lord, preached the gospel to the Jews in Cyrene, which is in modern day Libya (Acts 6:9). As a result, the descendants of Simon, who carried the cross for Jesus, and whose body was touched by Jesus' blood, heard the gospel and were saved.

This is why I believe the names of Simon's children, Alexander and Rufus, are mentioned in Mark 15:21: *"Then they compelled a certain man, Simon a Cyrenian, the father of Alexander and Rufus, as he was coming out of the country and passing by, to bear His cross."* I firmly believe that through the blood of Jesus, salvation came to his entire family.

In my own family, my mother was the first to receive salvation. I was next, followed by my brother and my father. I am certain that God gives salvation to the entire family when one person comes into the saving grace of Jesus Christ.

Application:

In the same way, we who have been touched by the blood of Jesus have the promise of salvation for our family. Believe with all your heart and declare every day about God's promise for your family salvation. The One who promised is faithful and His word will never fail. When our family is saved, like Joshua we can say, *"But as for me and my house we will serve the Lord"* (Joshua 24:15).

Prayer:

Dear Heavenly Father, You are the One who instituted family so that we would not be alone. You shed your blood to save us. You have promised that the same salvation I have received is for my family too. I intercede on behalf of my family. I pray for the salvation of all my family members according to Your Word. I pray for those who have not experienced your salvation, who have rejected you or have gone astray. I bind the devil who has blinded the eyes of my family. Let them see the light of Your gospel. Let them receive the protection and blessings that flow from the blood of Jesus. I ask all this in the faithful name of Jesus Christ. Amen!

Reflection:

Write the names of your family members and believe with all your heart that they will be saved.

How are you actively serving the Lord in your home?

The Blood of Jesus Bestows Mercy and favor

*"[So that we might be] to the praise and the commendation of His glorious grace (**favor and mercy**), which He so freely bestowed on us in the Beloved. In Him we have redemption (deliverance and salvation) **through His blood,** the remission (forgiveness) of our offenses (shortcomings and t respasses), in accordance with the riches and **the generosity of His gracious favor.***"

— Ephesians 1:6-7 (AMPC, emphasis added)

Key Point:

The blood of Jesus bestows the mercy and favor of God upon our lives. The mercy and favor of God will enable us to receive favor from the people of this world.

Message:

Several years ago, an evangelist came to India from America. Due to his ignorance of Indian law, he ended up getting detained by the government officials and faced certain charges due to his actions. A friend of mine, who was a pastor, asked me to intervene on behalf of this evangelist. So, I met with the concerned official. I explained that this gentleman was not a terrorist or drug dealer, but was genuinely serving the community through various noble causes. Though I was able to convince most of the officials to take a lenient view for his offense, there was one officer who was determined to see him penalized. I met with him several times at his office, but he bluntly refused my request.

I decided to meet the officer at his house. I called his wife, and she asked me to come meet him that very evening. That day, I happened to be fasting, and I was really tired. I hopped onto my motorcycle and drove to his house. As I was approaching my destination, the car in front of me stopped very abruptly. I swerved to avoid hitting the car and tried to drive around it. As I passed the car, one of the passengers opened his door and hit me. The impact knocked me down and flung the motorcycle away.

Anxious not to miss my meeting, I quickly got up, restarted the motorcycle and managed to reach the officer's house in time. When he opened his door, the officer was shocked at my appearance. I was covered in blood from the numerous cuts and bruises all over my body. He administered first aid and helped me calm down.

After I was comfortable, the officer asked, "Why are you so keen on helping this American?" I replied, "The man has helped many leprosy patients, widows, orphans and installed bore wells in many villages in our country. I want to help him in return." I still remember the look on his face when he saw me covered with blood. I believe the compassion he felt towards me that night, plus the favor of God upon my life, caused that man to change his mind towards the evangelist.

Proverbs 16:7 (NLT) says, *"When people's lives please the Lord, even their enemies are at peace with them."* We read in the Bible that Noah found grace (unmerited favor) in the sight of the Lord as he led a life pleasing to God. God chose Noah to build the ark, which became the vessel of salvation for Noah and his family from the destruction caused by the great flood. I strongly believe that God will render His favor to the body of Christ just before his second coming (Psalm 102:13,16) as He demonstrated His favor towards Israelites when they came out of Egypt (Exodus 12:35-36). We will now see how we can appropriate God's favor in our lives in this time.

The story of Isaac, Rebekah, Jacob, and Esau is one that deals directly with God's favor and blessing. In his old age, Isaac wanted to bless his older son, Esau. He asked Esau to go hunt and prepare a delicious meal to enjoy before he blessed him and died.

When Rebekah, Isaac's wife, heard this, she took Esau's favorite clothes and put them on Jacob. She positioned the skins of goats on Jacob's hands and neck. She prepared a meal of savory meat and bread, and told Jacob to take it in to his father. She wanted Jacob, her youngest son, to receive his father's blessing. Isaac was surprised that his son was able to prepare the meal so quickly. We read the following conversation between Isaac and Jacob as recorded in Scripture:

So he went to his father and said, "My father."
And he said, "Here I am. Who are you, my
son?" Jacob said to his father, "I am Esau your
firstborn; I have done just as you told me; please
arise, sit and eat of my game, that your soul may
bless me." But Isaac said to his son, "How is it
that you have found it so quickly, my son?" And
he said, "Because the LORD your God brought
it to me." Isaac said to Jacob, "Please come
near, that I may feel you, my son, whether you
are really my son Esau or not." So Jacob went
near to Isaac his father, and he felt him and said,
"The voice is Jacob's voice, but the hands are the
hands of Esau." And he did not recognize him,
because his hands were hairy like his brother Es-
au's hands; so he blessed him. Then he said, "Are
you really my son Esau?" He said, "I am." He
said, "Bring it near to me, and I will eat of my
son's game, so that my soul may bless you." So he
brought it near to him, and he ate; and he brought
him wine, and he drank. Then his father Isaac
said to him, "Come near now and kiss me, my
son." And he came near and kissed him; and he
smelled the smell of his clothing, and blessed him

and said: **"Surely, the smell of my son is like the smell of a field which the LORD has blessed"** (Genesis 27:18-27, emphasis added).

When we study this incident, we see that Isaac doubted. He wasn't entirely convinced that it was Esau that brought him the meat. He questions this—not once, but six times! In spite of this, Isaac still blessed Jacob. Do you know why?

Genesis 26 begins by telling us there was famine, caused by drought in the land. We are told that Isaac sowed and still reaped a hundredfold in the same year. God blessed him, and he became very prosperous. He had many animals and servants, but the Philistines envied him. They stopped up the wells dug by his father Abraham (Genesis 26: 12-15). As a result of this and other disputes, Isaac had to relocate several times. And at each new location he was able dig a well and find water (Genesis 26: 19, 21, 22 and 25). Isaac was able to identify the field that God had blessed with water, and tell his servants where to dig the well. According to Genesis 27:27, Isaac could smell the blessing of God on a field.

I believe that Isaac was able to smell God's blessing on Jacob in the same way he smelled the blessing of God on a field. This was why he went ahead and blessed Jacob in spite of his doubts. He knew the blessing of God was already on his son, whether it was Esau or Jacob. He blessed the one that God had already blessed.

Now, Jacob put on the clothes of his elder brother and the skins of goats when he went in to receive the blessing. Let me explain to you the spiritual significance of this act. Romans 8:29 implies that Jesus Christ is our elder brother. Revelation 19:13 says that the robe of Jesus was dipped in blood. Judges 16:17, 22 indicate that hair symbolizes the anointing. Like Jacob, when we put on the clothes of our older brother Jesus, dipped in blood, and apprehend His anointing, God will bless us even when we do not deserve it. *The blood of Jesus unlocks the favor of God in our lives.*

> *The blood of Jesus unlocks the favor of God in our lives.*

Application:

I have heard renowned preachers define mercy and grace as follows: Mercy is when we do not receive what we deserve (James 2:13). Grace is when we receive what we do not deserve. When we sin, we deserve to be punished, but through the blood of Jesus, God shows mercy towards us. Therefore, we escape punishment. When David sinned, he sought the mercy of God. By the mercy of God, when our sins are forgiven by the blood of Jesus, we have right standing with God, and that enables us to receive the favor of God in our lives.

Psalm 51:1-2 says, *"Have mercy upon me, O God, according to Your lovingkindness; according unto the multitude of Your tender mercies, blot out my transgressions. Wash me thoroughly from mine iniquity, and cleanse me from my sin."*

Because of our sinful life, we do not deserve anything from God. However, by His grace, we receive many good things from God, that are both undeserved and unearned (Ephesians 2:5-8). Like Jacob, though we do not deserve it, the blood of Jesus bestows the unmerited favor of God on our life.

Psalm 5:12 says, *"For You, O LORD, bless the righteous man [the one who is in right standing with You]; You surround him with favor as with a shield"* (AMP). What a wonderful privilege it is to receive the mercy and favor of Almighty God in our life! The blood of Jesus has earned that for us. Believe this truth, and enjoy God's mercy and favor in every day of your life.

Prayer:

Dear Heavenly Father, I cannot thank You enough for Your mercy, grace, and favor in my life. Many times, when I walked in the shadow of darkness, I thought that You had forsaken me. Now I understand that Your mercy and favor endure forever and Your blood has earned that for me. Now, by faith I apply the blood of Jesus on me, my family and all that concerns me. Your word tells me that your mercy and grace are new every morning. Let these follow me wherever I go. Help me to receive favor in the sight of authorities, coworkers, and others. I pray this in the incomparable name of our Lord Jesus Christ. Amen!

Reflection:

How can we realign our lives in order to walk in the favor of God?

In what ways has God bestowed favor in your life?

The Blood of Jesus Bestows Covenant Blessings

*"For **this is My blood of the new Covenant,**
which is shed for many for the remission of sins."*

– Matthew 26:28 (emphasis added)

Key Point:

The blood of Jesus has bestowed all the covenant blessings on us. Our rebirth in Christ has given us the right to tap into God's abundant blessings, and make us a blessing to others.

Message:

In the Old Testament, whenever a covenant was made between God and man, blood was shed to ratify the covenant. For instance, when God made His covenant with Abraham:

As for Me, behold, My covenant is with you, and you shall be a father of many nations. No longer shall your name be called Abram, but your name shall be Abraham, for I have made you a father of many nations. I will make you exceedingly fruitful; and I will make nations of you, and kings shall come from you. And I will establish My covenant between Me and you and your descendants after you in their generations for an everlasting covenant, to be God to you and your descendants after you. Also I give to you and your descendants after you the land in which you are a stranger, all the land of Canaan, as an everlasting possession, And I will be their God (Genesis 17:4-8).

God's covenant called for the circumcision of the foreskin of Abraham and his descendants. We read in Genesis 17:10-11, *"This is My covenant which you shall keep, between Me and you and your descendants after you: Every male child among you shall be circumcised; and you shall be circumcised in the flesh of your foreskins, and it shall be a sign of the covenant between Me and you."* From these verses, we can infer that blood has to be shed in order to enter into a covenant relationship.

When Abraham was one hundred years old, God blessed him with a son, Isaac. When Isaac was a boy, God tested Abraham. God asked him to offer his son as a sacrifice on a mountain in Moriah. Abraham obeyed God implicitly. He built an altar at the appointed place, laid his son Isaac on the wood for the burnt offering, and took up the knife to slay his son. Just then, an angel from heaven intervened saying, *"Do not lay your hand on the lad, or do anything to him"* (Genesis 22:12).

Now I would like to share an insight with you from Genesis 22:13-14, which says, *"Then Abraham lifted his eyes and looked, and there behind him was a ram caught in a thicket by its horns. So Abraham went and took the ram, and offered it up for a burnt offering instead of his son. And Abraham called the name of the place, THE-LORD-WILL-PROVIDE; as it is said to this day, 'In the Mount of The LORD it shall be provided.'"*

When the angel asked him not to do any harm to his son, Abraham *lifted* his eyes. Why did he lift up his eyes? In Genesis 15:5 we see the Lord taking Abraham outside and, saying, *"Look now toward heaven."* We also see the Lord speaking to Abraham in visions in Genesis 15:1, 17:1.

Genesis 22:13 says, *"Then Abraham lifted his eyes and looked, and there behind him was a ram caught in a thicket by its horns."* If he was looking up, how then could Abraham see a ram *behind* him?

I believe that when Abraham looked up, the Lord began speaking through visions to Abraham. The ram *behind* Abraham signifies that a ram would come *after* his days, in his descendants' time, to be sacrificed. Moreover, in Genesis 22:14, we see that the ram had already been provided when Abraham named the place as "The LORD will provide." Considering this was after the ram had already been sacrificed, he could have called the place "The LORD has provided." It is very clear that he was talking about the future. Spiritually speaking, I believe that this ram symbolizes Jesus, who was to be sacrificed for all mankind in *the future*.

Though the descendants of Abraham followed the command of circumcision, God's promises for these Israelites could not be fulfilled because of their sinful lives. The Israelites lived in bondage, fear and sorrow. That is why God sent His only begotten Son. Jesus fulfilled God's covenant with Abraham and made a new covenant with His blood.

> *To this day, through the new covenant of His blood, Jesus gives all blessings to anyone who accepts Him in faith.*

Through this new covenant, God opened the doors for the fulfillment of the old one with Abraham, regarding his descendants. *To this day, through the new covenant of His blood, Jesus gives all blessings to anyone who accepts Him in faith.*

Galatians 3:29 says, *"And if you are Christ's, then you are Abraham's seed, and heirs according to the promise."*

In a sense, Jesus Christ was a descendant of Abraham. Whoever receives Jesus as his or her own personal Savior, and is cleansed by His blood, has the blood of Jesus in him or her. Because of that blood, he or she becomes a descendant of Abraham. So, every promise given to Abraham and his descendants is ours too!

Application:

According to the new covenant made by the blood of Jesus, we can claim all the promises given to Abraham and his descendants. Galatians 3:14 says, *"That the blessing of Abraham might come upon the Gentiles in Christ Jesus, that we might receive the promise of the Spirit through faith."*

I would like to highlight some of the covenant blessings of our Lord promised to His children:

- The Lord your God will set you high above all nations of the earth.
- Blessed shall be the fruit of your womb, and the fruit of your ground and the fruit of your cattle. There shall be increase of your herds and the young of your flock.
- The Lord will cause your enemies who rise against you to be defeated before you. They shall come out against you one way and flee before you seven ways.
- The Lord will command the blessing on you in your barns and in all that you undertake.
- The Lord will establish you as a people holy to himself, as he has sworn to you.
- All the peoples of the earth shall see that you are called by the name of the Lord, and they shall be afraid of you.
- The Lord will open to you his good treasury, the heavens, to give the rain to your land in its season

and to bless all the work of your hands.
- You shall lend, but you shall not borrow.
- The Lord will make you the head and not the tail, and you shall only go up and not down.

The blood of Jesus not only confers all these blessings on our lives; it also makes us a blessing to others in order to fulfill the covenant that God made with Abraham and his descendants. What a great privilege it is! So, let us praise God for the blood of Jesus that has the power to bestow on us all the blessings of the covenant.

Prayer:

Dear Father in Heaven, You made an everlasting covenant with Your people. Jesus, Your Son, shed His precious blood to fulfill the covenant that You made with Abraham. Not only did You renew Your covenant, but You also brought us into Abraham's lineage through the blood of Jesus Christ. Thank you for this great gift, and for blessings that we receive through this covenant. Cleanse me by Jesus' blood and let all Your covenant blessings flow into my life. Bless me, so that I, too, will be a blessing to others. In the covenant-keeping name of Jesus Christ, I pray. Amen!

Reflection:

Have you ever thought that you are entitled to all the blessings stated in the Old Testament? Did you know that you claim them by faith in His blood?

In what ways have you seen God's blessings in your life?

The Blood of Jesus Imputes God's Love in Your Life

"In this the love of God was manifested toward us, that God has sent His only begotten Son into the world, that we might live through Him. In this is love, not that we loved God, but that He loved us and sent His Son to be the propitiation for our sins."

– 1 John 4:9-10

Key Point:

The blood of Jesus will help us love God and others in the midst of all our troubles.

Message:

The Bible does not say that God is full of love. It says that God IS love (1 John 4:8,16). You cannot separate God and love. Because of His great love, God sent His only Son, Jesus, into this world to die for us. Because of His great love, Jesus Christ went to the cross and shed His blood for us. Because of His great love, the Holy Spirit abides in us and guides us through this dark world.

I will never forget the year 2006—the year our family was adversely affected in so many ways. There were seven specific types of attacks on our lives. I was being threatened by a gangster, which negatively impacted our entire family. Then, my wife was transferred to a new office about one hundred miles from our home. A little later, my wife had a fall and dislocated her shoulder. She had to take a month off from work because of this injury. All of a sudden, our son was affected with shingles in his eye while he was writing his junior college final exams. In September of that year, my father had a heart attack and died. My wife fell again soon after this, and this time she ruptured her Achilles tendon. After the surgery to fix this, she was confined to bed for four months. She also lost a whole year's salary while she was recovering from sickness.

And to add to all this, our sixteen-year-old daughter Sharon died suddenly on November 30.

The day we buried our daughter, we had to carry my wife in on a stretcher because she was still bedridden. After Sharon's death, there were many false rumors about us. Some newspapers slandered me and tried to ruin my reputation. A Christian magazine published that I was a liar. I was deeply depressed. I was devastated. I had just lost my daughter, my wife was bedridden, and I was not sure whether she would ever walk again. People I considered friends were now judgmental. I was emotionally,

socially, and financially at the end of the road. The worst
blow was hearing a man of God say that my daughter did
not make it to heaven. It was more than I could bear.

During this time, I did the only thing I knew. I spent
almost all my time praying and reading the Bible. I thank
God for the people who stood by me and prayed for me
during this time.

One day as I was praying, our Lord clearly asked me,
"Son, do you still love me?" I responded, "Lord, do you
really love me?" With that question in mind, I flipped
through the Bible and I found out how much my Lord
loves me. Here is what I discovered.

- Jesus loves me even though I am a sinner (Romans 5:8).
- Jesus gave His life for me (John 3:16, 15:13; 1 John 4:10).
- Jesus' love towards me is everlasting (Jeremiah 31:3).
- Jesus' love redeemed me (Deuteronomy 7:8).
- Jesus' love made me God's child (1 John 3:1).
- Jesus' love made me joint heir with Christ (Romans 8:17).
- Jesus' love made me a king and a priest (Revelation 1:5-6).
- Jesus' love gives me victory (Romans 8:35-37).
- In his letter to the Ephesians, Paul asks them to grasp how wide, how long, how high and how deep is the love of Christ (Ephesians 3:18).

God's love towards man is beyond human comprehension.

Jesus called Peter, a fisherman, and for three years imparted His vision and teachings to him. Peter saw the

> *God's love towards man is beyond human comprehension.*

manifest presence of God upon Jesus on the mount of transfiguration. Peter witnessed Jesus performing several miracles. Peter even had a revelation about who Jesus really was, when others regarded Him as just another man. Peter said to Him, *"You are the Christ, the Son of the living God"* (Matthew 16:16). In spite of all of this, Peter denied Jesus, not once, but three times in one night.

Early that morning, Peter heard the rooster crow and remembered the words of Jesus, *"Before the rooster crows, you will deny Me three times."* Peter's heart broke when he realized his mistake. He wept bitterly and repented for his actions (Matthew 26:75).

After the resurrection, Jesus said to Simon Peter, *"Simon, son of Jonah, do you love Me more than these?" He said to Him, "Yes, Lord; You know that I love You." He said to him, "Feed My lambs." He said to him again a second time, "Simon, son of Jonah, do you love Me?" He said to Him, "Yes, Lord; You know that I love You." He said to him, "Tend My sheep." He said to him the third time, "Simon, son of Jonah, do you love Me?" Peter was grieved because He said to him the third time, "Do you love Me?" And he said to Him, "Lord, You know all things; You know that I love You." Jesus said to him, "Feed My sheep"* (John 21:15-17).

Though many conclusions can be inferred from the

above, I believe Jesus made it very clear to Peter that he should forget his past. Rather, he should accept Jesus' agape love for him—perfect, unconditional, sacrificial, and pure—and move forward in his life and ministry.

Peter tried to love Jesus in his own strength and failed miserably. But in his grace, Jesus helped Peter understand His love for him. This revelation of Jesus' love made Peter a very successful minister. He boldly preached the gospel to those who had crucified Jesus. He preached the good news to gentiles and government officials. God used him to heal the sick, bless the poor and even write a portion of the New Testament of the Bible. Ultimately, he died a martyr's death.

All these Scriptures gave me a fresh revelation of God's love for me. I relish the fact that His love is the gateway to fulfilling His destiny for my life. And so, in the midst of all my trials and tribulation, I decided to do what He wanted me to do with my life. I said, "Lord, thank you so much for helping me to understand your unfailing love for me. Help me to love you the way you want me to love you."

Our Lord made me understand that I cannot do anything about my past failures and disappointments. If I continued to hold on to my past, not only would I be miserable, but so would those around me.

A parent's love for the children is unconditional. They are united by blood. In the same way, when you are born again, there is a divine blood connection through Jesus Christ. That means God loves you regardless of your condition. Since His blood runs in your veins, you are able to love God and love others—which are the greatest commandments (Mark 12:29-31).

Romans 5:5 says that God's love has been poured out in our hearts through the Holy Spirit. Leviticus 8:30 says that Moses sprinkled not only the blood, but also the anointing oil. 1 John 5:8 says that the Spirit, the water, and the blood, are knitted together in the earth. This means where the Spirit of God is, the blood is also present, as they are interrelated. So, we can say, the blood of Jesus imputes God's love into our lives. And the more you meditate on Jesus' suffering on the cross, the more you will be driven to love Him. That love will flow from your heart and cause you to love others.

As I began to grasp God's love for me, God revealed himself even more in my life. In an amazing way, our Lord opened new doors of opportunity and began providing additional resources to do His work. Today, we run a children's home

> *I can truly say that in my life, God's love has never failed and it will never fail in your life either.*

in memory of our daughter. My television program is on some TV channels in India, as well as on the Internet. In addition to providing education for children of rural families, we support poor widows and gospel teams that travel from village to village sharing the love of Jesus.

The Lord has enabled me to write numerous books, which have been a blessing to many. He has opened doors for me to minister His Word in several continents. We have seen many lives touched, souls saved and baptized with the power of the Holy Spirit around the world.

Finally, and perhaps most importantly, the Lord revealed to me, through visions, dreams, prophecies, and through the Scriptures, that my daughter is in His loving hands.

The Bible says, *"Love is patient, love is kind. It does not envy, it does not boast, it is not proud. It does not dishonor others, it is not self-seeking, it is not easily angered, it keeps no record of wrongs. Love does not delight in evil but rejoices with the truth. It always protects, always trusts, always hopes, always perseveres. Love never fails"* (1 Corinthians 13:4-8, NIV).

I can truly say that in my life, God's love has never failed and it will never fail in your life either.

Application:

Jesus shed every drop of blood to reveal God's love towards you. Therefore, live a life that reflects God's love to others. The world longs for true love. Will you allow God's love to manifest in your life? Will you love your enemies? Will you do good to them? God shows no partiality (Acts 10:34). What He has done for me, He will do for you.

Prayer:

Dear Loving Heavenly Father, thank You for revealing Your everlasting love for me through Your Son Jesus Christ. My heart melts at the thought that the creator of the universe willingly gave His life to save me. Who am I that you are mindful of me, Lord? Help me understand the depth of Your love. Let Your love fill my heart and drive out all bitterness, anger and other negative emotions. Help me to reflect Your love to my enemies. Help me extend my hand to those in need. I pray this in the ever-loving name of our Lord Jesus. Amen!

Reflection:

How do you exhibit God's love towards others?

Is there any bitterness in your heart? Pray that God's love would replace any bitterness.

The Thirst of Jesus' Blood

"Therefore I will divide Him a portion with the great,
And He shall divide the spoil with the strong, Because
He poured out His soul unto death, And He was numbered
with the transgressors, And He bore the sin of many, And made
intercession for the transgressors."

− Isaiah 53:12

Key Point:

God's heart cry is for souls to be saved from the clutches of Satan. Our hearts should reflect the heart cry of God, and we should constantly endeavor to live for God, and reach out to people so that they turn to Him!

Message:

Today's verse clearly says that our Lord will snatch the spoils from the enemy's stronghold because He poured out His soul to death.

Jesus, from the garden of Gethsemane all the way to the cross, poured out His blood. Even at the very end when the Roman soldier plunged his spear in Jesus' side, he drew out a mixture of blood and water (John 19:34). This meant that every drop of His blood was shed en route to Calvary till there was nothing left! Leviticus 17:11 states that life is in the blood, and this blood makes atonement for the soul.

When we read the verse at the beginning of the chapter, we see that Jesus poured out His soul even unto death. This means that he poured out his very life; every drop of blood signified life, and, as each drop fell, His soul was also poured out. His blood, which was not marred by sin, became the atonement and the eternal sacrifice that would spare our souls from perdition. Today, Jesus stands at the right hand of God the Father interceding for us and working out the pardon of our sins so that we might inherit the Kingdom of God. The gruesome torture of hell is reserved for the devil and his angels. Even the worst sinner is not meant for hell but deserves to find pardon in the blood of Christ that was shed on the cross.

Satan, the ruler of this world, has blinded the eyes of the people and has kept them under his control. When Jesus came, He utterly destroyed the authority of Satan over our lives by His blood (Colossians 2:14-15). We win the war over sin and are set free from the clutches of Satan; when we repent of our sins and confess them, we find forgiveness.

Every repentant sinner is the "spoils of war" that is spoken of in the above verse. We, as sinners saved by grace, are the trophies of the great battle between good and evil. We are the *"prize"* that Jesus won on the cross.

Jesus said, *"No one can enter a strong man's house and plunder his goods, unless he first binds the strong man. And then he will plunder his house"* (Mark 3:27). We know who the strong man referred to here is. But what exactly is inside the strong man's house? In Luke 4:5-6, when Satan endeavors to tempt Jesus, Satan tells Him that all kingdoms (the people of the world), glory (worldly wealth) and power (authority) have been given to him! From this we know that Satan has authority over the people of the world, and over earthly things.

However, the resurrection of Christ made Him the victor over the worst enemy known to man—death. After His resurrection, Jesus said that He had been given all authority in heaven and on earth (Matthew 28:18). This simply means that as former prisoners of sin and death, who are now inheritors of eternal life, we have the authority in our life to overcome the attacks of Satan (Luke 10:19). Satan may still promise us the comfortable life—a life full of earthly riches—but we need to seek eternal life.

When we bind the forces of Satan every day, we overcome the "strong man" and we can claim the prosperity, power and authority that Jesus has already won for us.

Revelation 12:11 says that the most powerful weapon to overcome Satan is the blood of Jesus. My experiences can confirm this! The blood of Jesus is, without doubt, the most powerful weapon to bind the strong man, Satan, and take his spoils. By pleading the blood of Jesus, shackles and strongholds are broken so that captive souls are liberated for the Savior. *The blood of Christ is the most effective tool to win souls for the Lord.*

Whenever I am asked to preach at a revival meeting, I often go to the venue that morning, and by faith, I sprinkle the blood of Jesus on every seat there. A few years ago, there was a gospel meeting conducted by my friend in Andhra Pradesh, India. On the final day of the meeting, there was a tremendous presence of God that engulfed the arena. At the conclusion of the meeting, all the people on the stage suddenly rose to their feet and started to praise and thank God loudly. I did not understand the reason until the pastor told me the incredible testimony the next day.

In this town, there was a prominent man, a manager in a local bank. He was highly influential and well respected. He was, however, an atheist, and would often make fun of his believing wife and other Christians who professed the faith. On this particular day, at his wife's insistence, he reluctantly dropped her off at the venue where the meeting was being held. He then headed to the club for a drink. He returned a while later to find that the event was still on. Curious about "these crazy Christians," he

> *The blood of Christ is the most effective tool to win souls for the Lord.*

entered the arena and leaned against a wall, and in his heart, he began to mock those who were filled with the Holy Spirit. Suddenly, he felt someone tap his shoulder. Fear gripped his heart, as he knew that he was leaning against a wall, and so this was impossible. He closed his eyes and felt drawn to the stage. He knelt before the platform and surrendered his life to Christ that very evening. Hallelujah! The blood of Christ was not shed in vain. It works even today.

When Stephen was stoned to death, he did not ask God to avenge his enemies. Instead, he asked God to forgive them (Acts 7:58-60). This blood cry of Stephen reflected the heart cry of God–the thirst for souls to be saved. It was this cry that caused the conversion of Saul, who was once a persecutor of Christians.

Application:

We, as children of God, should have this same thirst for souls. Through His blood, Jesus as our high priest is interceding for us all the time. This same Lord has given us His blood as a tool so that we might liberate captives from the kingdom of Satan. The only thing He wants us to do is to thirst, like He does, for the souls of those who are headed to eternal damnation.

Jesus, in His time here on earth, walked among people of all kinds. He was not inhibited by their differences, but instead showed love and compassion even to the ones considered most unlovable. He reached out to the lepers and the social outcasts. He encountered the sick, lame, blind and those who were downtrodden. He even reached out to a demon-possessed man in the graveyard and set him free. He reached up to the teachers of the law like

Nicodemus and to gentiles like the Roman centurion. For God is no respecter of persons. Our race, religion, status or ranking is of no significance to Him. His only desire remains that our souls are won for the Kingdom.

We are all made in His likeness—irrespective of our differences—and He thirsts for all of us to enter into His salvation. Therefore, like our Creator, may we also reach out with an earnest thirst for souls. May we love the lost and needy, so that we can quench the heart thirst of Christ by offering unto Him a refreshing drink of souls. May the blood of Christ which sets captives free, display in our lives its power and dominion over sin, Satan, and the grave so that all men may know that Christ is Lord!

> *We are all made in His likeness—irrespective of our differences—and He thirsts for all of us to enter into His salvation.*

Prayer:

Dear Heavenly Father, I thank You once again for the blood that Your Son Jesus Christ shed on the cross for us all. I know that it is not your desire that even one soul should perish in the eternal flames of hell. It is Your heart's cry that every single soul should be pulled out of Satan's clutches. Let this also be the cry of our hearts. Let us thirst for the salvation of souls, just like You do. Let us not stand by and watch as our brothers and sisters head toward eternal damnation. I pray that You will use me as an instrument that will point people in Your direction so that they also may know Your saving grace! May my heart thirst for what Your heart thirsts for, always! In the saving name of Jesus I pray. Amen.

Reflection:

Do you have the compassion for the lost souls that compels you to reach out to them?

In what areas have you grown spiritually since coming to salvation?

The Blood of Jesus Gives Eternal Life

*"Most assuredly, I say to you, unless you eat the flesh of the Son of Man and drink His blood, you have no life in you. Whoever eats my flesh and **drinks My blood has eternal life** and I will raise him up at the last day."*

– John 6:53-54 (emphasis added)

Key Point:

The blood of Jesus has surely made a way for us to go to heaven, where we can live with Jesus. We don't need to fear death. We will all meet in heaven one day, and spend eternity praising God for all He has done!

Message:

In the beginning, the Lord God formed man from the dust of the ground and breathed into his nostrils the breath of life; and man became a living soul (Genesis 2:7). Death came due to the disobedience to God's word (Genesis

2:16-17). From that time, everyone born into this world has to face death one day. If you die today, where will your soul go? Have you ever thought about it? When a person dies, his physical body goes into the earth. But the actual person, his soul (mind, will, emotion), lives on for eternity—either in heaven or in hell. The Bible says, *"For the wages of sin is death, but the gift of God is eternal life in Christ Jesus our Lord"* (Romans 6:23).

The greatest free gift God has given to those who believe in Him is eternal life.

I want to help you understand how the blood of Jesus imparts eternal life into those who believe. In mathematics, we can see a simple principle of equal properties at work. If a=b and b=c, then a=c. With these equations in mind, I would like to explain certain things to you about the blood of Jesus.

The life of a person is in his blood (Leviticus 17:11). This means my life is in my blood and your life is in your blood; and the life of Jesus was in His blood. When we say, "the life of Jesus" we speak of the life of God. God has neither a beginning nor an end. He is ever living. *"The life was manifested, and we have seen, and bear witness, and declare to you **that eternal life which was with the Father and was manifested to us"** (1 John 1:2, emphasis added). This eternal life is in the blood of Jesus Christ. When a person truly repents and asks for forgiveness, by

> *The greatest free gift God has given to those who believe in Him is eternal life.*

faith the blood of Jesus comes into that person. When Jesus' blood comes, it brings with it the life of God, and that life is eternal.

To go back to our math equation, we see three elements of the blood equation. If we, those who repent and have faith, receive Christ's blood, and Christ's blood has the eternal life of God, then we too have eternal life. This is why I believe that when we have the blood of Jesus in us, we have eternal life.

When we partake of the Lord's Supper, we consume the bread that is symbolic of His body, and drink the wine that is His blood. We remember His suffering; His blood enters us and gives us eternal life. John 6:53-54 clearly tells us the same thing, that when we eat of the body and drink of the blood of Jesus, we receive eternal life. This is why people on their deathbeds often choose to confess their sins and participate in the Lord's Supper—because they know it can bring them eternal life.

The first time I visited America, one of my friends took me to a home meeting in Beverly Hills, California. As we were driving through the neighborhood, I started admiring the large, beautiful houses. My friend told me that many of the rich and famous lived in this area. When he started naming some of them, it dawned on me how much more important the people were than the houses they lived in. In the same way, we often give more importance to the house of our soul, our physical body, rather than the soul itself.

Beloved! If the blood of Jesus has washed your sins,

your soul is made pure. Beyond that, the precious blood of Jesus leads you into eternal life. A true Christian does not ever have to fear death. Everyone who is washed by His blood has the hope that, even after physical death,

> *The one who has promised is faithful; He will NEVER break His promise.*

they will live forever with Jesus. This is a gift from God that we have not earned by our works. Jesus has promised eternal life to all those who place their faith in Him, and who have His blood in them. Moreover, Jesus is the only one who promised that He would take us to the Father in heaven. *Jesus said to him, "I am the way, the truth, and the life. No one comes to the Father except through Me"* (John 14:6). *The one who has promised is faithful; He will NEVER break His promise.*

There are several verses in the Word of God that show that eternal life belongs to those who are in Christ.

- *"Jesus said, 'Verily, verily, I say unto you, He that believeth on me hath everlasting life,'"* (John 6:47, KJV).
- *"Jesus said to Mary, 'I am the resurrection and the life. He who believes in Me, though he may die, he shall live. And whoever lives and believes in Me shall never die. Do you believe this?'"* (John 11:25-26).
- *"O Death, where is your sting? O Hades, where is your victory? The sting of death is sin, and the strength of sin is the law. But thanks be to God, who gives us the victory through our Lord Jesus Christ"* (1 Corinthians 15:55-57).

The Scripture also says, *"For there is a happy end for the man of peace"* (Psalm 37:37, ASV). I can say that this is true of the death of my dear grandfather—after family prayer, he went to bed and he passed away.

In the book of Acts, we meet Stephen, the first Christian martyr who gave his life for the sake of the gospel of Christ. The Bible says that even when he was undergoing terrible suffering, while the people were stoning him, he could pray for his persecutors, as Stephen had the certainty of eternal life (Acts 7:58-60). Similarly, since the time of Nero, many martyrs have laid down their lives with peace and joy in their hearts for the cause of Christ. For a true Christian, death is not the end; rather it is the beginning of a glorious life with Jesus Christ forever. Because they had the assurance of everlasting life earned through the blood of Jesus, they were not fearful about the death of their mortal body.

Application:

The Scripture clearly says, *"I will ransom them from the power of the grave; I will redeem them from death. O Death, I will be your plagues! O Grave, I will be your destruction! Pity is hidden from My eyes"* (Hosea 13:14). Praise the Lord! He has redeemed us from death. Do you believe that Jesus can give you eternal life? Do you believe that there is power in communion table of the Lord?

Give your life to Jesus, and His blood will surely bring eternal life and you will live in heaven with Jesus forever!

Whether or not I get to meet you in person while on earth, I am sure I want to see you in heaven! Amen.

Prayer:

Dear Father God, I thank You for the precious blood of your son Jesus Christ that was shed 2000 years ago to give me eternal life. I truly repent of my sins and accept you as my savior of my life. Please write my name in the book of the Lamb. Your word says, "Though I walk through the valley of the shadow of death, I will fear no evil; for You are with me." Please take away all fear of death. Help me leave this world happily and come to you at the appointed time. In the eternal life-giving name of Jesus Christ, I pray. Amen!

Reflection:

Are you sure of going to heaven if you depart from this world now?

Did you know that eternal life can only be found through relationship with Jesus Christ?

Part Six

The Role of Jesus

30

Jesus as Mediator, Advocate, and High Priest

"But when this priest had offered for all time one sacrifice for sins,
He sat down at the right hand of God"

– Hebrews 10:12 (NIV)

Key Point:

Through His blood, Jesus intercedes for us as Mediator, Advocate, and Priest in heaven, even today! He will not let us down.

Message:

After He ascended to heaven, Jesus sat down at the right hand of the Father. He returned to the glory He had before His life on earth (John 17:5). Even today, He continues in His role as King of Kings and Lord of Lords (1 Timothy 6:15), as well as His eternal role as the second Person of the Godhead (Matthew 28:19). As Jesus sits in glory, He acts as our Mediator, Advocate, and High Priest.

His Role as Mediator

"For there is one God and one Mediator between God and men, the Man Christ Jesus" (1 Timothy 2:5).

A mediator attempts to settle a dispute between two parties. God had a dispute with us because of our sin. God hates sin, which causes us to be separated from Him. Without a mediator, we would have become an object of God's wrath and would have been destined to spend our eternity in hell, separated from God. But there is Good News!

There is a Mediator between God and man—and that is Jesus Christ.

Those who place their trust in His finished work on the cross are reconciled to God by His precious blood (Colossians 1:20). They are at peace with God (Romans 5:1).

His Role as Advocate

"My little children, these things I write to you, so that you may not sin. And if anyone sins, we have an Advocate with the Father, Jesus Christ the righteous" (1 John 2:1).

A few years ago, I visited an attorney in Chennai, India, who specialized in clearing loans. Each of the clients at his office was confident that the attorney would win his case and resolve their problems. Later, the attorney told me that his basis for arguing cases like these was to prove that his client had meager income, and then he would negotiate a settlement with the creditor.

If a good attorney can argue and win cases for his clients in a court of law, with only a few documents and with little or no supporting evidence, just imagine what our Advocate in heaven, Jesus Christ, can do for us through His blood!

Remember, Satan is the accuser who accuses us before our God day and night (Revelation 12:10). When we commit a sin, Satan immediately takes us to the court in heaven to accuse us. But when we truly repent, Jesus our Advocate puts forth the argument that we, in Christ, have already been absolved. He explains and reasons that when we accepted Jesus as our Savior, we became

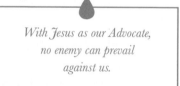

With Jesus as our Advocate, no enemy can prevail against us.

part of His body, and He was already punished for our transgression. His blood that was shed is the evidence of that punishment. How then could God, the Judge, punish us, Jesus' clients, again when the penalty has already been paid?

As our Advocate, Jesus not only pleads on our behalf, sparing us from the punishment we deserve, but He also defends us from the attacks of the devil. When the devil attacks us in any manner, Jesus Christ with His precious blood is there to defend us.

With Jesus as our Advocate, no enemy can prevail against us.

His Role as High Priest

"Seeing then that we have a great High Priest who has passed through the heavens, Jesus the Son of God, let us hold fast our confession" (Hebrews 4:14).

A close friend of mine, who is a pastor in a slum area in Chennai, shared a wonderful testimony with me. He told me that whenever he went to a small grocery store near the slum area where he lives, he always shared Bible verses with the storeowner who was not Christian. After a while, this storeowner fell into debt and could not repay his loans. In desperation, he went to a secluded place to commit suicide.

Suddenly, every Scripture the pastor had ever shared with him came to his mind. He returned to his store and told my friend what had happened. The pastor said to him, "Jesus died for you, why should you die?" These words really touched his heart and he accepted Christ. The pastor also prayed for him and his business. Our Lord amazingly brought him out of the debt, and today he is a blessed man.

In Numbers, at the end of chapter six, we find what is known as the Priestly Blessing. *"And the LORD spoke to Moses, saying: 'Speak to Aaron and his sons, saying, 'This is the way you shall bless the children of Israel. Say to them: 'The LORD bless you and keep you; The LORD make His face shine upon you, And be gracious to you; The LORD lift up His countenance upon you, And give you peace.' So they shall put My name on the children of Israel, and I will bless them,'"* (Numbers 6:22-27).

From these verses, we can conclude that God blesses His people through the prayers of his priests. If the prayers and sacrifices of earthly priests can bring blessings, imagine what blessings the prayers and sacrifice of Jesus, our heavenly High Priest, can bring into our lives.

In the Old Testament, the priests interceded on behalf of the people by offering sacrifices as required by the Law. One of these priests was selected as the High Priest. His responsibility was to enter the Most Holy Place once a year, on the Day of Atonement, and sprinkle the blood of the sacrifice on the Mercy Seat. But these sacrifices covered the sins of the people only temporarily until Jesus Christ came to the earth to take away the sins of all mankind (Hebrews 7:26-27).

Jesus, our High Priest, offered Himself as a sacrifice for our sins.

Jesus, Who is our High Priest now in Heaven, started his ministry at the age of 30 as required for a priest to serve in the tabernacle (Numbers 4:3). Anointed by God (Matthew 3:16; Luke 3:22), His Words and prayers brought blessings in many people's lives. After His resurrection, He entered the Most Holy Place and sprinkled His own blood on the Mercy Seat (Hebrews 9:12), bringing eternal redemption to all who come to God through Him.

In addition to this, when Jesus came into this world, He was one hundred percent God and one hundred percent man. As a man, He faced the same temptations and weaknesses that we face; therefore, He can empathize with our struggles (Hebrews 2:18, 4:15). He knows exactly how to intercede on our behalf (Hebrews 7:25).

Jesus is called our Great High Priest (Hebrews 4:14), and through His blood we can boldly come to the throne of grace to obtain mercy and find grace to help us in our time of need (Hebrews 4:16).

Application:

Although Jesus shed His blood two thousand years ago, He still uses His blood in His roles as Mediator, Advocate, and High Priest to bring blessings into our lives. He spares us from wrath, defends us against the Enemy, and intercedes on our behalf. Because our High Priest "ever lives to make intercession for us" we can be assured that He is working all things for our good. What a loving God we have!

Prayer:

Dear Almighty God, I thank You for sending your Son Jesus into this world to save me. What an awesome privilege it is to have Jesus as my Mediator, Advocate and High Priest! Lord Jesus, thank You for Your various roles in heaven on my behalf. Thank You for bringing me to God. Thank You for defending me before God and protecting me from the devil. Thank You for being my High Priest and bringing blessings into my life. Help me stay assured that You are standing in the gap for me, so that I am never discouraged. Help me remain faithful to You. In the immutable name of Jesus Christ, I pray. Amen!

Reflection:

Why do you have anxiety about your day-to-day problems?

In what areas are you not trusting God?

Conclusion

Jesus Christ, the Son of God, came into this world as a Son of Man. Although Jesus took on the form of a mere mortal, He led a holy life without sin. However, his enemies falsely accused him.

In the garden of Gethsemane, Jesus was in great agony and prayed earnestly. His sweat became like great drops of blood falling down to the ground (Luke 22:44). Then the multitude, sent by the chief priests and religious leaders, came with swords and staves. They arrested Jesus and took Him to Caiaphas, the high priest, to be interrogated by the religious leaders. When Jesus said that He was the Son of God, they immediately condemned Him to death. They mocked Him, hit Him on the face, and spat on Him before taking Him to Pontius Pilate.

Pilate commanded the Roman soldiers to scourge Jesus. The whip they used consisted of a short handle and several long heavy leather straps. Embedded in each strap were pieces of metal and bone to add weight, and for greater impact. The pieces of metal and bone protruded from the strap long enough to form sharp hooks.

With full force, the Roman soldiers whipped the shoulders, chest, back, legs, and face of Jesus. At first, the heavy straps penetrated the skin, but as the blows continued, they cut deeper and deeper into His flesh. Each time the whip was drawn back to deliver another blow, the metal and the bone hooks grabbed and tore off pieces of skin and flesh (Psalm 129:3). It is also possible that the whip would have struck Jesus on the face, plucking flesh and hair from His cheeks (Isaiah 50:6).

The soldiers assigned to the governor took Jesus into the governor's palace and brought down the entire brigade. They braided a crown from the branches of a thorn bush and placed it on his head. Historians describe the crown as made of small flexible branches covered with long thorns. These thorns were very strong, extremely sharp, and capable of making deep wounds. When the soldiers placed the crown upon His head, the thorns penetrated His scalp. The soldiers then put a rod in his right hand for a scepter, and bowed before him and mocked him, saying, "Hail, King of the Jews" (Matthew 27:27-29).

The guards who slapped and punched Jesus were not ordinary people. They were very strong, trained soldiers. Their blows would have been powerful and capable of causing severe injury. Then they spat on Him and hit Him on the head with a rod, again and again (Matthew 27:30, NIV; Micah 5:1-2). Each subsequent blow on Jesus' head would have driven the thorns deeper and deeper into his scalp (Matthew 27:30; Mark 15:19). Jesus was stripped of His clothing and beaten mercilessly. Then they dressed Him in a red toga and mocked Him further. The soldiers then took Jesus to Pilate to be presented to the Jews (John 19:2-5).

While this was going on, the blood from Jesus' wounds would have soaked into the robe He was wearing and would have begun to clot. This would have caused the robe to stick to His body. After Pilate delivered Jesus up to be crucified, the soldiers tore the robe off His body (Mark 15:20). Not only would this have caused excruciating pain, it would have also plucked skin, flesh, and even hair from His body (Isaiah 53:7).

They forced Jesus to carry a rugged cross through the streets of Jerusalem, and at Golgotha they nailed his hands and legs with strong nails (Psalm 22:16; John 20:25; Luke 23:33). Even after Jesus had died, a soldier pierced His side with a spear to determine whether He was dead or still alive (John 19:34).

Hundreds of years before all this happened, the Prophet Isaiah had a revelation about how our Lord's body would be mutilated, and how His face would be marred. We can read this in the book of Isaiah chapter 53 where it says, *"There is no beauty that we should desire Him. He is despised and rejected by men."*

Jesus is the Son of the Almighty God! Why did Jesus

allow Himself to be placed in the prisoner's dock? Why did He take all those insults upon Himself? Why was He beaten? Why did He endure the cross? Why did He give up His life on the cross, allowing His own innocent blood to be shed? *Beloved! The answer is simple: He shed His blood so as to bestow eternal blessings on you and me, and on all mankind.*

In Hebrews 9:16-17, we read that a testament or will comes into force only after the death of the testator, that is, the person who wrote the will. The new covenant of Jesus Christ is likened

> *Beloved! The answer is simple: He shed His blood so as to bestow eternal blessings on you and me, and on all mankind.*

to a will and testament. After Jesus' death, the power of His blood activated the New Covenant, and as a result, we receive an eternal inheritance (Hebrews 9:15).

As promised by our Lord in Zechariah 13:1, we now have a fountain opened for all God's children for cleansing from sin and unrighteousness.

There is indeed power in the blood of Jesus Christ!

The Covenant Blessings in the Blood of Jesus

Under the old covenant, the blood of animals and birds was applied by sprinkling it with hyssop. Under the new covenant, we apply the blood of Jesus through our spoken word. *"For with the heart one believes unto righteousness, and with the mouth confession is made unto salvation"* (Romans 10:10). Psalm 107:2 clearly urges a redeemed person to *confess* his redemption.

Therefore, having now learned of the blessings earned by Jesus through His blood, let us believe and profess the following statements, and inherit all of the blessings covenanted to us! Make theses declarations continuously in order to apprehend all these blessings in your lives (Psalm 35:27). I personally believe that the more you declare God's Word, it will quicken the process of obtaining the results in your life.

- The precious and holy blood of Jesus Christ, the Son of the Living God, has redeemed me.
- The everlasting power in the blood of my Savior has removed all my addictions and set me free.
- I am forgiven, cleansed, and sanctified by the blood of Jesus Christ.
- I am born again, and my conscience has been purged; I am a new person in Christ Jesus.
- The blood of Jesus has removed all the spiritual barriers, as well as the attire of sin. I now have direct access to the throne of God. I have the privilege to worship Him in the beauty of His holiness, sit with Him in the Heavenly Places and hear His voice.
- I am the righteousness of God, and the favor of God is around me like a shield.
- I am a partaker of the covenant blessings of Abraham through the blood of Jesus Christ.
- All my debts have been paid and my curses broken. I will be a source of blessing in this world.
- The blood of Jesus has bestowed upon me the revelations of the Word of God and the power to create. I will create new things for the glory of God.
- I am a king and priest in the kingdom of God. Satan and all my worldly problems are under my feet.
- I smear the blood of Jesus upon myself, my family, my business and on all my belongings. No harm will befall me, and no plague will come near my tent.

- All schemes and strategies of Satan, which are against my family and me, have been disarmed and destroyed by my Savior on the Cross.
- No witchcraft power or sorcery has any effect on my life. No weapon formed against me can harm me.
- By the power of the covenant blood of Jesus, everyone in my family will be saved.
- My Lord has carried all my sickness and infirmities on the cross. By His stripes I am healed.
- I have the peace of God in my heart, in my home and family, and in all my endeavors.
- I will be a victor and more than conqueror through Him who loved me. The joy of the Lord is my strength.
- God's love is imputed in my heart, and I will reflect His love to the hurting.
- I will be a soul winner for my Savior who saved me from going to hell, and from the bottomless pit.
- I will dwell in the house of the Lord forever through the sacrifice of the Lamb of God.

Amen.

Acknowledgments

First, I offer my thanks to my Lord Jesus Christ, who entrusted me with these revelations and gave me the grace to write and publish this book.

I express my heartfelt thanks to my dear wife Elizabeth, my children Mervyn, and Sharon (late), my daughter-in-law Sheryl M. Samuel, my father Mr. C. I. Ebenezer (late), my mother Mrs. Bessie Ebenezer, my brother Ruban and his wife Esther, and also to my mother-in-law Mrs. Sakkubai for their constant love and support.

I extend my sincere thanks to Mrs. Seline Augustine, Mr. John Victor (late), Mrs. Rebekah John, Mr. Prakash Williams, Mrs. Marsha Thompson, and Mr. Charles Stanley, who gave me invaluable suggestions and ideas from time to time.

I am grateful to my office staff, who all toil along with me in my work.

I thank all our partners for their prayers and earnest love and support for our Lord's work.

I am thankful to all the staff of the Fedd Agency, who helped me to produce and publish this book.

– Samuel M. Ebenezer

Endnotes

1. Ross, and Mary Hunter. "The Year the Scarlet Thread Stopped Turning White - the Importance of the Historical and Cultural Context." January 1, 1970. http://evbibletalk.blogspot.com/2017/01/the-year-scarlet-thread-stopped-turning.html.
2. Strong's Hebrew: 817. (asham) -- offense, guilt. Accessed December 10, 2019. https://biblehub.com/hebrew/817.htm.
3. Strong's Hebrew: 817. (asham) -- offense, guilt. Accessed December 12, 2019. https://biblehub.com/hebrew/817.htm.
4. Strong's Greek: 38. ἁγιασμός (hagiasmos) -- consecration, sanctification. Accessed December 12, 2019. https://biblehub.com/greek/38.htm.
5. Strong's Hebrew: 2483. (choli) -- sickness. Accessed December 10, 2019. https://biblehub.com/hebrew/2483.htm.
6. Strong's Hebrew: 4341. makob) -- pain. Accessed December 12, 2019. https://biblehub.com/hebrew/4341.htm.
7. See note 5

If you have been blessed by this book,
introduce this book to others,
and be a blessing.

TO CONTACT THE AUTHOR:

211, BAY SHORE ROAD,
BAY SHORE, NY 11706.
631-665-5241

E-MAIL: SAMEBY1959@GMAIL.COM